THE MINDFUL LEADER

TEN PRINCIPLES
FOR BRINGING OUT
THE BEST
IN OURSELVES
AND OTHERS

Michael Carroll

TRUMPETER
BOSTON & LONDON
2007

Trumpeter Books
An imprint of Shambhala Publications, Inc.
Horticultural Hall
300 Massachusetts Avenue
Boston, Massachusetts 02115
www.shambhala.com

9 8 7 6 5 4 3 2 1

First Edition

Printed in the United States of America

♾ This edition is printed on acid-free paper that meets
the American National Standards Institute Z39.48 Standard.

Distributed in the United States by Random House, Inc.,
and in Canada by Random House of Canada Ltd.

Designed by Gopa & Ted2, Inc.

Library of Congress Cataloging-in-Publication Data

Carroll, Michael, 1953–
The mindful leader: ten principles for bringing out
the best in ourselves and others / Michael Carroll.—1st ed.
p. cm.
Includes bibliographical references
ISBN 978-1-59030-347-4 (hardcover: alk. paper)
1. Leadership. 2. Meditation. 3. Mind and body.
4. Motivation
(Psychology) I. Title.
HD57.7.C3683 2007
658.4'092—dc22
2007016272

To my teachers, past and present,
and the noble lineage of bodhisattva-warriors

The challenge of warriorship is to live fully in the world
as it is and to find within this world,
with all its paradoxes, the essence of nowness.

—*Chögyam Trungpa Rinpoche, Eleventh Trungpa Tulku*
of the Kagyu Surmang lineage of Tibet

Face reality as it is, not as it was or as you wish it to be.

—*Jack Welch, former CEO of General Electric*

CONTENTS

PART THREE: BRINGING OUR FULL BEING TO WORK

PART FOUR: PRACTICES AND EXERCISES

THE MINDFUL LEADER

THE TRADITION OF THE MINDFUL LEADER

I T'S TUESDAY AFTERNOON, and in forty-eight hours, you and your team have to deliver the final budget for the new product line. Two of your team members have to catch a flight in eight hours, and they are working feverishly to complete their piece of the plan. The senior product designer is leaving to pick her children up at school, and the finance department is on the phone requesting—well, *demanding*— some preliminary numbers for the CEO to review before the day is out. And you . . . well, you're trying to keep the team focused and coordinated in an atmosphere that feels like a pressure cooker on steroids. And then your boss enters the room and says, "I want everyone to stop what they're doing right now and give me your full attention. Set your laptops aside, hang up the phones, put the spreadsheets away, and stop editing the PowerPoint presentations."

Now, such an entrance will grab our attention no doubt, because it hints of some ominous business, indeed. But then your boss says, "Now that I have your attention and we've stopped working, let's sit here for a moment . . . just quietly sit here and do nothing at all."

For many of us, such a scenario would be absurd. Here we are in the midst of a fast-paced project, trying to meet a tight deadline and handle some unpredictable demands, and suddenly we are asked to "stop and just sit here"?! While such a suggestion may appear unacceptable or even insulting, it is exactly what is happening in many work settings throughout the United States and around the world. People are taking time to simply "sit still" and practice what is widely known as mindfulness meditation. Let's review just a few examples:

▶ Confronted with the distressing fact that over 60 percent of medical interns were exhibiting symptoms of severe burnout, Dr. Craig Hassad of Monash University Medical School in Melbourne, Australia, taught his doctors to meditate.

▶ Companies such as Raytheon, Proctor & Gamble, Unilever, Nortel Networks, Comcast, and many law firms have offered their employees classes in mindfulness meditation.

▶ When Harvard Law School sponsored a conference of practicing attorneys to investigate why lawyers tend to get trapped in adversarial mind-sets and suffer from remarkably high rates of depression, it began the conference by practicing mindfulness meditation.

▶ "Protecting and Serving without Fear," a seminar offered to law enforcement agents in Madison, Wisconsin, taught the attending police officers how to meditate.

▶ Executives such as Bill Ford Jr., the chairman of Ford Motor Company; Michael Stephen, the former chairman of Aetna International; Robert Shapiro, the ex-CEO of Monsanto; and Michael Rennie, the managing partner of McKinsey, meditate and consider such a practice beneficial to running a corporation.

So, while such a suggestion as "stop and sit still" may appear absurd, many of us are, in fact, doing just that in a wide variety of business settings. But why? Why would we—or anybody, for that matter—stop and sit still for fifteen to thirty minutes or even an hour? Recent research seems to be giving us many reasons: repaired immune systems, heightened emotional intelligence, reduced anxiety and depression, sustained levels of joy and satisfaction—even gaining control over some of the most distressing emotional disorders. Scientific studies are indicating that practicing mindfulness is just plain healthy, giving us plenty of reasons, indeed.

But despite all these apparent benefits, maybe there is another reason why it makes sense to stop and sit still—something that has nothing to do with relieving stress or achieving anything at all. Maybe the millions of people throughout history who practiced mindfulness meditation were rediscovering something about being human—something so simple and so deeply profound that it could only be understood *intimately* rather than scientifically; something so direct and authentic that it demands vulnerability and heart rather than ambition and achievement. *The Mindful Leader* is about exploring this intimacy of sitting still and learning how such a simple act could transform our complicated and demanding modern workplace.

My journey into today's workplace started in the 1980s on Wall Street, where I was one of thousands of determined young people arriving in New York in search of success and personal fulfillment. And Wall Street was a fantastic place to get started: a world filled with passion, brilliance, and ambition—ever on the hunt for profit and seeking "business leaders" who could lead the way.

As my career unfolded, I was invited to attend various leadership seminars and felt honored to be considered a candidate for becoming a leader. At the time, I wasn't sure what being a business leader meant. I knew it involved making decisions, galvanizing teams, assuring quality, and strengthening productivity. But I also had the vague feeling that becoming a business leader was about power, ambition, and success; it was about moving "up"—rather than "down and out"—which seemed the right direction to take.

At the same time, I was also studying Buddhist meditation under the guidance of Tibetan teachers, foremost among them Chögyam Trungpa Rinpoche, the renowned master. Unlike today, when meditation and yoga have become mainstream, in the 1970s and 1980s, the workplace did not consider studying such topics the brightest thing to do. If the subject of meditation or Tibetan Buddhism came up at work, people would often ask the strangest questions: "Is it true that meditation can teach you to fly?" or "Do you have a secret mantra such as 'Om' that can place mystical powers into crystals?" Or even more disturbing, "I've heard about that tantric sex stuff. What is it like? How often to do you get to do that?" And on occasion, there would be snidely dismissive smiles, as if those who meditate were profoundly out of touch with the "adult real world" of business and work. There were so many misconceptions about meditation at that time that, generally, I kept my spiritual path to myself, discussing it rarely and only with my closest colleagues.

Of course, my Buddhist training had nothing to do with learning to fly or meditating on crystals. In fact, my training was quite rigorous, requiring daily meditation, frequent solitary retreats, and regular study. And as my Buddhist education naturally mingled with my corporate training, I gradually came to recognize that there was more to leadership than pursuing success or making weighty decisions. My Buddhist training revealed a different model of leadership not based on ambition, will, and achievement but inspired by wisdom, gentleness, and authenticity. While Wall Street was training me to become a business leader, my Buddhist teachers were training me to become a bodhisattva-warrior.

I, for one, never considered myself a candidate for the leadership job of a bodhisattva. Traditionally, bodhisattvas were considered spiritually accomplished beings who could overcome arrogance, aggression, and greed and fully realize their humanity. Bodhisattvas were noble leaders who inspired the best in others and worked to help those in need. And while I wanted to achieve such lofty goals, I pretty much considered myself a "wannabe"—or, at best, a "gonnabe"—bodhisattva. Over time, however, I came to realize that such leadership was far more down-to-earth than I had imagined and that the workplace, with all its ingenuity and passion, had, in many respects, lost its way and could benefit greatly from the vision, skill, and leadership of bodhisattva-warriors.

Now, aspiring to be a bodhisattva leader, whether at work or elsewhere, can be tricky business, especially if we have some preconceived notion about making the world a better place. Such spiritual aspirations can often create more confusion than clarity, so it's always prudent to be a bit suspicious of such things—to slow down and get a realistic picture of what we are trying to do.

And when we *do* slow down and get a realistic picture of

what we are doing, we discover that too often we are speeding past our lives rather than actually living them. Finishing the homework, getting into college, arriving at work on time, scheduling appointments, meeting the targets, landing the promotion—it's as if we have been managing life as a project rather than truly living it. And it is right here in the midst of this speed and hectic activity that we may catch a glimpse of what it means to lead the life of a bodhisattva-warrior. For even a split second, we may notice the remarkable and vivid fact that we have fully arrived in our lives and we are being invited to appreciate a world in need of our help. It's as if the entire world is inviting us to stop speeding through life—to sit down and be still and fully appreciate our circumstances. Such a glimpse is more than just a hippie notion of "be here now" or of being a good girl or boy. It is an invitation from reality to become fully human.

Throughout my business career, this glimpse has always brought my bodhisattva aspirations down to earth. This gentle invitation to stop, sit down, and be still—to notice that we have already arrived in our lives—has offered me and thousands of others a mindful way of life. And central to the bodhisattva-warrior tradition is the possibility that such mindfulness can revitalize our workplace and cultivate *mindful leaders* who could accept the invitation to become fully human and, in turn, lend a hand to a world in need of help.

This book imparts some of the basic principles and practices for becoming just such a mindful leader and for bringing such leadership into the organizations where we work. In one sense, there is nothing new here, since all that is presented is drawn from the twenty-five hundred–year-old Buddhist tradition of the bodhisattva. But at the same time, applying these principles in our modern workplace presents us with unique challenges and difficulties.

When we pause to appreciate work, we discover some true marvels. We can communicate around the world through all kinds of clever devices and travel comfortably to any destination. We produce medicines to soothe our suffering, plentiful food to nourish us, and educational institutions to train and inspire. Cotton cloth, soap, eyeglasses, watches, and music CDs—the list of advances is endless. And each day, we build this astounding world as doctors, librarians, sales managers, scientists, teachers, truck drivers, farmers, parents, psychologists, and fast-food servers. Each of us leads and contributes in our own way, and together we build a world full of wonders.

Yet with all our progress and success, we also find ourselves in a world filled with unprecedented suffering. Sixteen thousand children starve to death every day, and 100 million people are without homes. Even our marvels can morph into tragedies: more than twenty thousand nuclear weapons are hidden throughout the world, and 4.6 million people die each year from air pollution.[1] If we pause to truly appreciate the circumstances of our livelihood, we discover that we have fashioned a world that offers great gifts but also demands our help.

This book is about how we can wake up to this challenge: how we can appreciate our good fortune and contribute, both at work and throughout our lives in general. In part 1, "Inspiring the Best in Ourselves and Others," we will explore an expanded way of leading that is not just a matter of being in charge or making things happen. Instead we will examine how to lead beyond arrogance, fear, and resentment and in turn inspire the best in others. Learning to open up to our daily experience and discover a willingness to "be" counterbalances our incessant drive to "achieve"—and this ability to be present in the moment is a natural wisdom that lies at the heart of being a mindful leader.

In part 2, "The Ten Talents of a Mindful Leader," we explore in detail how the simple act of sitting still can cultivate the leadership talents needed to revitalize our workplace. By practicing mindfulness meditation, we step past concepts and begin to express poise, courage, humility, and more—*if* we are willing to engage life on its terms rather than ours.

In part 3, "Bringing Our Full Being to Work," we examine how to engage our livelihood without hesitation or doubt through becoming "synchronized": in harmony physically, mentally, and emotionally. By synchronizing with our work, we rediscover our ability to be authentic, confident, and dignified and, almost magically, realize a powerful possibility: because we are inseparable from what we seek to influence, our ordinary daily behaviors may be far more potent than we think.

Finally in part 4, "Practices and Exercises," we explore traditional contemplations for cultivating mindful leadership. Such practices reveal that ordinary activities such as doing our job well, taking a walk in the woods, or raising our family with joy and care are not isolated incidentals, but instead form the foundation for building a positive and decent world. By working with these practices and exercises, we reclaim our natural wisdom and humanity.

For my part, engaging this workplace challenge mindfully and honestly has been a lifelong pursuit, and I have had the good fortune to be patiently trained by men and women from both the corporate world and Tibetan Buddhism. In both cases, my teachers have been exacting, the circumstances ideal, and my progress always a bit clumsy and resistant. I have learned from Tibetan masters and warehouse clerks, Zen roshis and schoolbook sales reps, Buddhist nuns and CEOs. Corporate America taught me about initiative, ambition, conflict, and results. Buddhism taught me about discipline, compassion, toughness, and skill. Each tradition had its unique way of grinding down my arrogance and insecurity and of cultivating my wisdom and confidence.

Over time and after many hard-earned lessons, these two traditions blended together and taught me one of the most valuable lessons in embracing the marvels and suffering of the workplace. In a sense, it is the basic rule for becoming a mindful leader, and all the practices and advice offered throughout this book can be distilled down into this single guiding principle:

> More often than not, seeking success for ourselves proves pointless and shallow, whereas seeking success and inspiration for others almost always delivers prosperity and well-being right into our hands.

This book is about making this principle come alive in our workplace—moving it from mere words to inspired personal action. And for those who choose to follow the path of the bodhisattva-warrior and cultivate the talents of a mindful leader in the workplace, I offer you a small wish: may you reclaim your natural leadership talents and extend such well-being to all you encounter.

PART ONE

INSPIRING THE BEST
IN OURSELVES AND OTHERS

As workplace leaders it seems that we are always trying to grow the business, meet the deadline, close the deal, and finish the project. And the speed and pace can be intense—getting it done faster, better, cheaper, and smarter. Such a style of leadership with all its ambition and energy has its benefits no doubt, but it also has a profound blind spot: in our relentless pursuit of "success," we too often forget to live our lives. When we lead a career that is sharply focused on being more successful, more admired, or just more comfortable, we can deceive ourselves into neglecting the world around us. We end up managing our lives like projects rather than actually living them. Consequently, for mindful leaders, cultivating this ability to *be* at work and throughout our lives is not just a nice idea or an interesting thing to do. Rather, by learning to *be* at work we discover how to stop kidding ourselves and respect the world around us. In the next several chapters we will explore the importance of learning to be at work—to *open* respectfully and realistically to our workplace as it unfolds in the present moment.

1

OPENING UP TO
WORKPLACE REALITIES

THE KINDS of leaders we encounter at work are generally what we call "top-down" leaders. We are all pretty familiar with this approach. There is the boss who has the "top" job and tries to get others "down" in the organization to do things. Small organizations such as medical teams and big organizations such as governments all have a leader at the top and others down below who are expected to follow. All of us at times are the leader and at other times the follower, and when it's our turn to lead, we work hard to get results. Surprisingly, becoming the boss at the top is usually more distressing than we expect, but nonetheless, we do our best to get the job done. While overly simplistic, this is the kind of leadership we normally encounter at work, and we tend to take such an approach pretty much for granted.

This kind of top-down leadership can be quite effective for managing organizations. Setting priorities, allocating resources, directing strategy—these and much more can best be done when we, as leaders, have a wide view from atop an organization. And when top-down leadership works, we all feel pretty good. We know what's expected of us, we have a clear sense of purpose, and we all pull in the same direction. But things don't always go so smoothly at work, and instead of pulling in the same direction, we can sometimes feel as if we have lost our way: we can feel "misled" and a bit discouraged, as if a burdensome and limiting "lid" were placed on top of us and our workplace.

Lids are common at work: unreasonable deadlines, rude colleagues, careless managers, onerous bureaucracy, frivolous demands—unfortunately, the list is long and familiar. Such lids are permitted to cover organizations when we, as leaders, lose our perspective and become out of touch with the realities of getting the job done. Instead of taking a wide, realistic view of work, we mistakenly hurry through our circumstances, overlooking advice, chasing deadlines, ignoring business facts, and frantically pursuing success. And despite all our good intentions, such a narrow, determined view drives us to put lids of pointless pressure on ourselves and others—demanding results rather than inspiring them, chasing opportunities rather than inviting them, insisting on respect rather than earning it. In the end, when lids are placed on organizations, we can find ourselves losing patience with our lives and in turn trying to conquer or dominate our work rather than accomplish it.

A doctor who manages a thirty-five–person dermatological medical center had come to one of my recent mindfulness meditation seminars in order to "unwind and get some perspective." She was physically fit, gracious, with a quick and winning smile—a doctor/surgeon of some fifteen years and decidedly *burned out*. As she told her story, she had begun her career as a dermatologist with great enthusiasm, inspired to build a medical practice dedicated to helping people. And she and her two partners, working hard for more than ten years, had achieved just that: a medical center equipped with the best technology, employing dozens of professionals, serving hundreds of patients daily. But, despite her success, she wanted to quit. Her partners squabbled, employees gossiped, and vendors cut corners. Overhead was more than twenty-five thousand dollars weekly, and malpractice insurance made it difficult to earn a profit. But most disturbing was how she felt she had changed from an inspired doctor to a short-tempered taskmaster. Work had become a burden and she, part of the problem, inflicting her frustration, frenzy, and disappointment on others. Despite all the business challenges, this doctor knew that she had lost perspective and was placing a lid on others, stifling the team's natural enthusiasm and focus. She was "fed up with the whole mess" and was considering a new line of business—leading hikes in the Colorado Rockies.

Throughout the weekend, many seminar participants recognized themselves in the doctor's story: the pressure to meet unreasonable demands, the stress of managing overly complex processes, the challenge of assembling a successful partnership. Some found themselves leading with an air of frenzy; others found themselves relying on data rather than insight and spreadsheets rather than hands-on experience. Such pressure and stress had pushed some of them to feel, like the doctor, under siege, increasingly rushed, tense, and unfocused, while putting on a game face.

Now, we didn't solve the doctor's problem during this weekend seminar—no weekend seminar could. But we did recognize in no uncertain terms how top-down leadership can lose its way and exhaust an organization, placing lids of senseless pressure on colleagues, organizations, and ourselves.

While such lids may be familiar to many of us, they are also a most bedeviling, pervasive, and unintended feature of our modern workplace. Hundreds of studies have documented the effects: 18 percent of full-time American workers are considered "workaholics," working more than fifty hours a week —up from 13 percent in 1999;[1] panic attacks, chronic worrying, and depression have increased by 45 percent in the United States over the past thirty years;[2] 1 million American workers are absent from work each day due to stress.[3] Many organizations work quite hard trying to remove these lids in order to encourage trust, candor, and mutual respect—often with limited results. There is no blame here, of course. We all create the lid to some degree—boss and subordinates together. Most leaders I have met throughout my career are often dumbfounded at how people in their organization *feel* pressured to keep their mouths shut and avoid risks. And most employees are equally dumbfounded at the fact that their leaders seem to be in the dark about the pressures to conform and not rock the boat. Everyone to some degree is well meaning; everyone to some degree is out of touch. And all of us to some degree create the lid.

From a Buddhist point of view, however, removing the lid of pointless pressure and regaining a realistic view of work is a vital spiritual challenge if we intend to lead a confident and inspired life. As workplace leaders, our intention is not to create pressure cookers for our colleagues, and none of us wants to stew in our own juices. While top-down leadership has many benefits, Buddhism does not permit us to view livelihood simply from the top down, nor can we wait for someone else to take the lead in contributing to our world. In fact, for Buddhists, learning to become a leader who can inspire and build a decent world without lids is at the very heart of living a spir-

itual life, and traditionally, to become such a leader requires us
to travel what is called the bodhisattva-warrior path, or the way
of the mindful leader.

LEADING FROM THE "INSIDE OUT"

As a college student in the 1970s, I befriended a young man
who made his living as a Pennsylvania Turnpike toll collector.
At the time, I considered his job fascinating: sitting in a small
box for hours on end making change for people as they paid
their taxes struck me as poetic—kind of like witnessing an endless stream of human dramas framed by car windows. Of
course, he clued me in to the facts: car exhaust, heat and cold,
frustrated commuters, and cramped work environments made
for some difficult times. But what truly fascinated me—and
apparently fascinated the New Yorker enough for it to publish
an article about my friend—was that he was tremendously
cheerful when doing his job, and many of his customers
brought this to the attention of the turnpike authority. He had
a most peculiar workplace habit that seemed to get everyone's
attention: he gave a piece of candy to each customer he encountered, accompanied by a big smile and a heartfelt "Have a good
day." Apparently, this had some impact on the thousands of
commuters who traveled past his window week in and week
out. Truckers got a chuckle, families waved good-bye, frustrated businesspeople breathed a brief sigh of relief—and in gratitude, some even took the time to thank his employer for his
generosity. And I remember my friend's enthusiasm and pride
when his picture appeared in the New Yorker—his head peering out from his toll booth with a goofy grin on his face and a

piece of candy in his hand. He felt he had made a substantial contribution to his world, and I, for one, agreed and could feel his inspiration quite viscerally.

Now, on the surface, such a gesture as offering a piece of candy to people while they pay their taxes may seem uneventful—perhaps a bit sweet and well intentioned, but not particularly pertinent to the topic of business leadership. Handing out candy has little to do with growing market share, striving for commercial excellence, or creating global opportunities. For the mindful leader, however, what is at play in this simple story is the very seed we seek to nourish—the essence of leadership itself.

Over the centuries, thousands of instructions have been offered by many skillful Buddhist teachers on how to cultivate the heart of a leader. Mastering such instruction is quite demanding and can take an entire lifetime—actually, many lifetimes, according to past teachers. But despite these demands, cultivating such leadership within ourselves and within organizations is very doable and straightforward—maybe even as simple as giving someone a piece of candy. In fact, mindful leadership is tremendously practical because it rests on a simple yet profound insight that expands the entire notion of leadership altogether: *all human beings instinctively want to offer their best to others and in turn inspire others to do the same, and this can be done by anyone, anywhere, anytime—even in a highway toll booth.*

Mindful leadership teaches that this instinct to inspire the best in others is completely natural—utterly human—and is at the very heart of being a leader. A child charming a smile from a parent, a neighbor hosting a spring outdoor barbecue, a world leader planning for the future, or a smiling toll taker offering a piece of candy—all are leaders in their own way, offering a part of themselves in order to inspire others.

From the standpoint of a top-down approach to leading, the fact that a toll taker could inspire others or that a barbecue could unfold as a leadership event may seem trivial or completely off the mark. But for the mindful leader, such simple human gestures hold the very secret of successful leadership. For here, in offering a smile or a piece of candy or a plan for curing cancer, this kind of leadership is the foundation—the core—the vital impulse that drives authentic leadership, which is less about leading from the top down and more about leading from the *inside out:* offering to others a part of ourselves that inspires. From this perspective, top-down leadership need not lose its way and become a lid when it understands and embraces this simple fact: each and every one of us, by the very fact of our humanity, is capable of leadership and responsible for leading—*from the inside out.*

THE PATH OF OPENING

Typically, when we think of leading, we think of guiding and instructing others, pointing the way, setting direction. And, surely, these activities are what leaders do. Yet for the mindful leader, leading from the inside out requires a primary act—a fundamental human gesture that must take place first and foremost, before any leader can guide or direct or point the way. According to the tradition of the mindful leader, a leader must first *open*—step beyond the boundaries of what is familiar and routine and directly touch the very people and environment he or she intends to inspire. Leading others requires that we first open to the world around us.

Many business leaders may find such an approach a bit peculiar. It's hard to imagine overhearing leaders in the boardroom saying to one another, "Hey, why don't we all open up to one another? You know, lead from the inside out." Such a view of leadership may appear a bit soft. Flowers and windows open, not leaders. Leaders make stuff happen; they accomplish goals. For mindful leaders, however, opening is not merely "a nice thing to do"—behavior that can be practiced at an off-site management session or during a game of Twister. Opening is how we become available to what is actually going on—how we become realistic about our circumstances, abandoning our *version* of reality for experiencing reality itself. Opening introduces us to how things *are* instead of how we want them to be. Consequently, opening is the primary and indispensable act of leaders because it requires that we fully understand and appreciate our circumstances *first* before we act.

I recall once waiting for an appointment in an executive reception area of a *Fortune* 100 company, and on the wall was an impressive photograph of the Atlantic Ocean. A lighthouse in the photo shed its guiding beam across the waves and shoreline, and the caption read, "Vision is not seeing things as they are but as they will be." I couldn't help running the first part of the saying over and over in my mind: "Vision is not seeing things as they are . . . Vision is not seeing things as they are. . . ." For the mindful leader, such "vision" is blindness, and focusing on the future without facing reality as it exists is choosing to be lost. I remember thinking to myself as I left the appointment,

"I wonder how that picture and trite phrase even got up there on the wall." And I could not help but think, "Maybe no one has even noticed it's there!"

Of course, we understand what the phrase is trying to get at. As leaders, we naturally want to improve our world, creating clever devices and beautiful spaces that are helpful and inspiring to others. We want to make the world a better place, so to speak. But seeking to make the world a better place without *first* appreciating the world as it is produces all kinds of problems. Rather than permitting the facts of life and the melody of circumstances to guide and educate us, we end up putting a lid on the experience, stifling the world with *our* views, *our* priorities, *our* vision—*our* hopes and *our* fears.

I recall a story shared with me by a publishing colleague about a New York CEO who was leading a team in acquiring a portfolio of medical magazines. The financial characteristics of the properties were quite attractive, with 25 percent profit margins and solid positive cash flow, and the executive was keen on making them part of his growing publishing business. After some research and preliminary due diligence, it came time for the CEO and his acquisition team to meet with the magazines' owner, and the meeting was arranged in the acquiring company's fancy boardroom.

As planned, the owner of the medical magazines and his lawyer arrived on time and, after a few cordial introductions, took their seats across the table from the CEO and his eight-person acquisition team to discuss the possibilities of joining forces. Before any business began, the CEO set a rather strange stage for discussion:

"Before we get into the details of this deal, let me ask you a very basic question," he remarked, looking directly at the owner. "Before this meeting, I asked my business development guy here to go downstairs and purchase your magazines at our magazine kiosk, and I'll remind you that it just so happens that our magazine store is one of the best stocked in the world, offering a wider array of magazines than 97 percent of all magazine kiosks." He paused for effect.

"And do you know what he found? Not one of your magazines is available for sale. Not one. So let me ask you a basic question: why would I want to spend millions of dollars to acquire your magazines and you can't even get them onto the magazine rack for purchase?" And the CEO sat back with a smug grin on his face.

The owner was a bit taken aback, not so much by the question as by the display.

"Well, it's a good thing that you didn't find my magazines in your kiosk downstairs," he calmly remarked. "My magazines are purchased by neurologists, brain surgeons, oncologists, and osteopathic physicians—and the likelihood that they would be wandering around in your building is pretty slim." The owner paused as quiet discomfort filled the room.

"My properties are what are called trade publications—they are highly focused and technically driven for specialized physicians and nurses. My magazines are not consumer publications, which is what you'll find downstairs. I sell subscriptions, not circulation, which is why my business is so profitable and its cash flow so rich."

Needless to say, the CEO was embarrassed—but not because he didn't know what he was talking about, which would have been perfectly appropriate. The CEO embarrassed himself because he was not open—open to meeting a potential new partner, open to learning new views of publishing, open to "not knowing"—open to just about anything that might happen. Instead, the CEO crudely put a lid on his world and ambushed his potential partner with *his* vision, *his* concerns, *his* opinions. Rather than be genuinely open, he chose one-upmanship; rather than curiosity, he chose arrogance; rather than extending a hand, he chose pretense. Being open in this circumstance would have been tremendously practical, but the CEO chose to hide beneath a lid.

Such clumsy attempts at leading are not unusual in business, and too often, leaders are actually expected to behave with such aggression, placing lids on circumstances. But as we can see from our embarrassed CEO, when we lead from the top down without openness, we can get out of touch, ignore the facts, and misunderstand our circumstances. We try to build *our version* of reality because we are not dealing with reality itself. When we try to influence our world without first appreciating it, we end up in a lighthouse on the edge of the Atlantic Ocean "not seeing things as they are" but as the way we want them to be—trying to manipulate our world into an artificial experience tinged with aggression.

JINPA: THE WISDOM OF VULNERABILITY

The primary act of mindful leadership, then, is to open—to fully appreciate our circumstances *before* we seek to influence or act upon them. When we are willing to open to our world before we act, we not only learn what we need to know, but equally important, we express a vital, innate intelligence that is sharp, flexible, and unassuming. At such moments, we view our workplace without any lenses, undistracted by *our* priorities, *our* preferences, *our* vision of the future. Instead, we grasp directly the full measure of our present circumstances, recognizing opportunities, appreciating others' views, acknowledging difficulties, and even delighting in the natural grace and flow of the moment. Such open intelligence, however, demands that we drop any pretense or strategy. Who we are and how we want to be perceived, what we want to accomplish and how we want to get there, become unimportant. In short, *we* become irrelevant.

By dropping our point of view—indeed, our identity altogether—we discover that to lead from a place of openness is to be vulnerable: undefended, engaged, and raw. At times, such vulnerability can be freeing because we stop wrestling with our personal schemes and anxiety and simply expose ourselves to our world. Yet conversely, such vulnerability can also be terrifying, since there are no familiar emotions or clichés on which we can rely for comfort or reassurance.

The Tibetan word for this vulnerable openness is *jinpa,* which means "complete generosity," and traditionally, cultivating jinpa is considered the basic practice of the mindful leader. It is how we learn to generously offer ourselves to others without making ridiculous demands or placing lids on situations. When we express jinpa—when we are intelligently open and vulnerable—we create the opportunity to genuinely lead and inspire others.

The suggestion that we lead by being vulnerable may seem absurd. Typically, we think that leaders should be equipped with all kinds of armor—invincible and potent, able to withstand the slings and arrows of workplace competition and hostility—and that being vulnerable at work means being weak, inadequate, shamefully flawed. For the mindful leader, however, the vulnerability of jinpa is not an inadequacy but a wisdom that is poised, skillful, and astute. The Olympic figure skater who flawlessly executes a double open axel understands the wisdom of vulnerability. The classroom teacher who pauses to soak in a child's anxious resistance before reacting understands this wisdom. The manager who genuinely listens to the disgruntled employee, the attorney who drops an adversarial mind-set, the martial artist at her ease, the orchestra conductor fully engaged—each understands the wisdom of jinpa's vulnerability.

On one of my consulting assignments, I was asked by a lead scientist to help her understand why members of her R & D staff were so intimidated—so unwilling to speak their minds and discuss vital issues openly. I spent time listening to many medicinal chemists and biologists, computer scientists and lab experts, and discovered a culture in which candor was clearly lacking. There were many reasons why people were reluctant to speak their minds, of course. But one most intriguing discovery truly defined the dilemma.

Essentially, these R & D scientists, like all scientists, wanted their experiments to succeed. Wedded to highly demanding processes and insisting on exacting rigor, they were trained to seek certainty, but *emotionally,* they desired the satisfaction of success with all its recognition and acclaim. By their very nature, however, these particular R & D efforts involved frequent failure—and there was the rub. Intellectually, the scientists could accept failure if their research showed that a particular compound did not perform according to plan. Emotionally, however, to admit such a thing required the courage to be *vulnerable*—vulnerable to the emotions associated with failure; vulnerable to likely criticism, second-guessing, and even doubt. And since frequent failure was a given, such emotional vulnerability was, in fact, an essential and necessary part of the territory. Unfortunately and somewhat understandably, the scientists were distinctly uncomfortable feeling vulnerable. On the surface, they behaved as if they were open to the facts of failure, but underneath, they were closed to the emotional realities of disappointment, discouragement, and doubt. During R & D meetings, dialogue was more about protecting oneself, proving a point, or defeating an argument than listening, considering options, or speaking candidly. People were more worried about covering their bases than engaging in productive dialogue. And, of course, being wary and defensive in such a way only provoked the very conflicts and tensions everyone wished to avoid. The emotional openness required for candid discussion and vital learning was absent, and the resultant culture was hesitant, lacking resilience and nerve. The lead scientist's challenge, therefore, was to model jinpa—the "wisdom of vulnerability"—encouraging the members of her team to set aside their resistance and hesitation and express themselves openly.

Over many months, she met with team members individually and in small groups, inviting candor—welcoming all remarks—praise, criticism, and suggestions. She gradually dropped much of her own resistance to irritating insults and second-guessing—embracing conflicts rather than treating them as nuisances. R & D review meetings were no longer intellectual wrestling matches but gradually started being managed more openly, with opinions being invited more widely and everyone encouraged to listen fully before probing for weak points. And while work continues to this day on strengthening the openness within the organization, much progress has been made, and in the lead scientist's own words, "The fear level in my organization has clearly been reduced, both by my actions and by stabilizing R & D as a whole." What was required in this R & D business was for each scientist to open from the inside out and emerge unguarded to discuss his or her research candidly—both successes and failures, certainties and hunches. The challenge was to engage the *seeming* emotional threats from a standpoint of vulnerability rather than defensiveness, which required courage and daring—total exposure.

Whether we are a lead scientist, a CEO, or an Olympic figure skater, when we lead from a place of total exposure, we discover that we are being authentic. We are not trying to win anyone over or guard our point of view. We are not sugarcoating our experience with trite pleasantries or arming ourselves with rusty emotional knives. Instead, we are simply open to whatever occurs, which inspires others to express such openness as well. Such vulnerability can have a powerful and lasting impact on organizations, promoting a common sense of collegiality, respect, and decency. Yet this wisdom of vulnerability is nothing particularly extraordinary or fantastic; such openness is not the stuff of PowerPoint presentations or management seminar exercises. The wisdom of vulnerability arises as an utterly human moment that can inspire a simple smile or rousing applause or even have such momentous consequences as saving a nation from disaster.

Few Americans know that in 1782, in the midst of the American Revolution, the Continental army mutinied. For all intents and purposes, the Continental Congress in Philadelphia had abandoned its army to suffer in miserable conditions. Soldiers were left unfed, ill-clothed, underequipped, and unpaid, and the officers of the Continental army repaid such lack of loyalty with an ultimatum spelled out in the "Newburgh Address," which essentially said to Congress, "Either care for your army properly or we shall take things into our own hands and march on Philadelphia."

No one appreciated the dangers of a potential military coup more than the army's commander, General George Washington, and he moved swiftly to deal with it. And not surprisingly, it was a simple gesture of vulnerability that turned the tide, preventing the mutiny and saving a nation.

Historical record tells us that on March 15, 1782, in the midst of the crisis, General Washington attended a meeting in a large assembly hall with hundreds of his officers in New Windsor, New York. As circumstances would have it, he arrived unexpectedly and alone, without bodyguards or entourage, which was quite unusual, since the British were working tirelessly to kidnap the general. For many years, through many trials, the troops of the Continental army remained fiercely loyal to General Washington and deeply respected him as a leader and patriot, but on that day, as he walked to the podium, the general faced hundreds of angry, frustrated, and hostile men. A bit unnerved, he read from a carefully prepared speech appealing to their patriotism, their military bearing, and even their pocketbook. But George Washington was an ineffective public speaker, and his pleas fell on deaf ears. The officers had not been moved and remained angry and mutinous.

As a last resort, the general had brought along with him a letter from a congressman that pledged to address their grievances, and he pulled out the handwritten note and began to read it aloud. The letter was hard to see in the darkened meeting room, however, and after stumbling through the first paragraph, the general paused and clumsily put on a pair of reading glasses. As the story has been told, many in the crowd began to mumble, taken aback because no one had ever before seen their tough, distinguished general wear frail, ill-suited eyeglasses. What happened next was witnessed by Lieutenant Samuel Shaw and recorded in his journal.

According to Lieutenant Shaw, the general fumbled with his glasses, trying awkwardly to position the reading spectacles on the bridge of his nose while holding the letter, and said, "Gentlemen, you must pardon me; I have grown gray in your service and now find myself going blind as well."[4]

This brief spontaneous remark—a simple gesture of vulnerability from a loyal soldier—touched the heart of each man in the room. "There was something so natural, so unaffected, in his appeal that it rendered it superior to the most studied oratory; it forced its way to the heart," wrote Shaw in his journal. General Washington's simple gesture was jinpa—total openness—and it instantly reminded all his assembled officers that they shared a profound dignity as patriots and soldiers. They had glimpsed in a flash the noble, authentic fiber of their general—a man who had given up everything to lead them—and just as suddenly, they were inspired to drop their anger and fear and express their own nobleness as well.

According to Shaw, some men trembled visibly, and many broke down, crying uncontrollably. Several comrades consoled one another, hugging like brothers. Apparently, General Washington was startled by the reaction as well and later wrote his officers thanking them for the "affectionate sentiments expressed" toward him during that difficult moment in history. After he left, the meeting ended calmly with little discussion, and the threat of a coup d'état ceased. And history records that

General Washington and his army remained united and not only received the much-needed support from Congress but went on to win the Revolution and establish the United States as a free democracy.

As a leader, George Washington had many outstanding traits: administrative brilliance, political savvy, patriotic passion, military vigor, and commercial astuteness. Yet what galvanized a nation to fiercely admire and trust him and truly distinguished him as a great leader was his openness—his willingness to be vulnerable and express his humanity in simple, authentic ways. Such openness—time and again—had a profound impact on his troops, his fellow American patriots, and the Continental Congress, repeatedly inspiring them to act on their most noble impulses. His officers trusted him on that fateful day in 1782 because he was open and vulnerable first and foremost.

In the tradition of the mindful leader, being open and vulnerable—whether we are a highway toll taker, a research scientist, or a noted general—is how we break the habit of placing a lid on ourselves and others. But opening is just the beginning of a greater journey; it is the first step into a world of larger possibilities and greater responsibilities. In fact, by opening, we discover the possibility of inspiring the very best in others and living a dignified life. But to do so, we must first face some powerful ironies and attend to our arrogance, aggression, and fear.

2

OVERCOMING SELF-DECEPTION: FOUR PARABLES

THOUSANDS OF ARTICLES have been written on how and why Enron, the multibillion-dollar Texas energy conglomerate, orchestrated its dismal failure. Opinions vary: third-rate investment strategies, incompetent management, lack of accountability, greed, arrogance, stupidity. The list is long, and most opinions seem to hold some kernel of truth. But what Enron's failure really came down to—what set in motion the thousands of astounding blunders—was that Enron's key leaders, such as Messrs. Skilling, Fastow, Lay, and others, had perfected the art of self-deception. Having built a successful track record in the natural gas business, these leaders became enamored with becoming something greater and more impressive: masterminds of a "New Economy," in which a single company could buy and sell just about anything—oil, pulp, water, broadband capacity, wind, even pollution. And coming from "masterminds of the future," business schemes that would have been deemed bogus at best in other organizations were saluted as the work of geniuses. In order to maintain the pretense, Skilling, Fastow, Lay, and others spent a lot of time kidding themselves—ignoring business facts, silencing objections, speaking in code, and fast-talking auditors. When analysis told a gloomy story and the markets would not respond, when pricing strategies proved disastrous and investments in ventures such as broadband shriveled, they focused on improvising PR strategies, *not facing reality.* They had become masterminds of the future rather than the present, and the rest is criminal history.

This art of self-deception is common throughout the business world, however, and from the perspective of the mindful leader, such self-deception is the direct result of closing up rather than opening to our workplace. In fact, for mindful leaders, self-deception is the singular challenge for all leaders at all levels in all organizations because it is how we behave as cowards, undermining our efforts to contribute to our world. We may think that our greatest workplace challenges are more concrete, such as implementing a new automated order-input system or securing a lease renewal at a reasonable rate. But how we behave as cowards at work—how we ignore facts, prefer expediency over substance, dress up hollow ideals, overreact to criticism, and author our own frustration—is a far more immediate leadership challenge, since it damages everything we aspire to achieve.

Traditionally, exploring self-deception and its underlying ironies often involves the skillful use of metaphors, poems, and stories, and the tradition of the mindful leader is rich with such tales. Beginning with the teachings of the Buddha more than twenty-five hundred years ago, metaphors such as a deer struggling in a net, a monkey grasping fruit in a bottle, an ox that refuses to be tamed, and many more have been used to illuminate self-deception's subtleties. This is not to say, of course, that self-deception at work should not be dealt with through straightforward, sober management. Setting clear priorities, making realistic demands, and inspecting results closely are how we learn to welcome facts rather than paint a picture of false success and status. But in the tradition of the mindful leader, fully appreciating the root cause of our dilemma requires that we contemplate some subtle and unpleasant spiritual ironies, and the expansive language of metaphor has proved quite effective for doing so over the centuries.

The following four stories are meant to do just that: illuminate the underlying reasons why we deceive ourselves as leaders, examine our role in the problem, and provide a perspective for moving forward. Such stories are meant to be contemplated and revisited over time, permitting their underlying lessons to change and inspire us. In the end, the stories are meant to point the way and hint at possibilities—to provide a vision for stepping beyond our cowardice and becoming mindful leaders who can open to workplace challenges rather than author self-deception.

1. A FARMER AND HIS CHILDREN
THE IRONY OF CHASING FALSE HOPES

Probably the most frustrating workplace irony for many of us is how we relentlessly pursue success but never seem to arrive at being successful. Of course, there are millions of successful people—Nobel Prize winners, college graduates, loving parents. But for a variety of reasons, so many of us do not *feel* successful even when we achieve much of what we are striving for. Particularly at work, we can find ourselves searching for wealth, recognition, and accomplishment, yet year in and year out, no matter how much we achieve, there's still something that seems to elude our grasp. The famed Greek fabulist Aesop shed some light on this dilemma more than twenty-six hundred years ago in a short tale entitled "A Farmer and His Children":

> A farmer, at death's door, wishing to impart to his children an important secret, called them to his deathbed and said, "My children, I am about to die. I would have you know, therefore, that our vineyard contains a hidden treasure—a treasure I have cherished all my life. Dig and you, too, will find it."
>
> When their father died, the children took spade and pitchfork and turned the soil of the vineyard over and over again in their search for the treasure, which they were told lay hidden in the vineyard. For weeks and weeks, they toiled, breathlessly searching every inch of the land. Finally, the children ended their search in frustration, for they had found no treasure. But to their surprise, the vines, after so much thorough digging, produced a bountiful, lush crop of grapes such as had never been seen before.

Like the farmer's children, we are all, in one way or another, looking for treasure at work: the promotion, new assignment, salary increase, recognition, big bonus. At times, it's as if we sense that work holds the winning number to life's lottery, and each day we toil in hopes of hitting the jackpot.

Yet like the farmer's children, most of us come up empty-handed. At times, work's disappointments can feel like a cruel joke. No matter how hard we work, no matter how much success we achieve, no matter how secure or celebrated we feel, it never seems enough. We work the fields of our jobs each day

in search of treasure, and too often we come home feeling unful-
filled, frustrated, and weary.

But Aesop's tale reveals a profound spiritual irony to our frustration: in mistakenly searching for a treasure that does not
exist, we overlook the good fortune being cultivated right
within our grasp. Like the farmer's children, we rush to get
somewhere else—to become more secure or more successful
or more wealthy—and in our rush, we overlook where we are:
we fail to notice that a great and bountiful harvest is unfolding *as we work.*

In so many respects, Aesop's tale reveals one of the great workplace contradictions that we face each day: *"success" tells us to
hurry up, find the treasure, get to the goal, whereas "work" tells
us to slow down, attend to the details, appreciate what is needed.*
And the task of trying to achieve both often feels impossible.

According to Aesop's tale, the "success" that we are rushing
to grasp does not, in fact, exist: misunderstanding the situation, we find ourselves chasing false hopes. The so-called treasure that lies hidden in the vineyard is nothing other than the
vineyard itself, yet mistakenly, we find ourselves desiring
something more fabulous and miraculous—more job security,
more wealth, more prestige—a treasure that will change our
lives, solve all our problems, and free us from our toil. But such
treasure—such success—does not exist.

Luckily, although there is no treasure, there is a bounty to
be found in the very act of our labor itself. If the farmer's children had realized this, their breathless turning of the soil need
not have been so frenzied, for they rushed past the actual experience their father had so cherished—they missed the joy of
their labor.

Of course, we could say that the farmer's children would

never have tilled the soil so vigorously unless they were searching for a treasure. But such a cynical approach to work is unnecessary. We need not lie to ourselves and chase after false hopes in order to be productive. We can care for our vineyard thoroughly and properly without the frustration of pursuing false hopes. We need not see ourselves as circus monkeys who perform only when tempted with enticements and charades.

And so it is, with this brief fable, that Aesop helps us glimpse how we, as workplace leaders, ironically author our self-deception, presenting us with a most compelling challenge, indeed:

> Can we stop chasing the false hopes of success and instead pay attention to the work itself—shaking off our blindness, arrogance, and worry and appreciating our job as it unfolds right before our eyes?

For the mindful leader, then, Aesop's challenge is to fully appreciate where we are at work and abandon our rush to get somewhere else that we hope will be more secure, more successful, or more amazing. And in so doing, we may discover a confident joy in our labor—a bounty that may open us up to our workplace and save us from the painful irony of chasing false hopes.

2. THE VICTIM'S DOORWAY
THE TRAP OF PRAISE AND BLAME

No matter what we do at work, someone, somewhere, sometime will eventually criticize us for our actions. Such criticism can range widely, from helpful feedback to destructive gossip, and one of the most subtle and pervasive forms of leadership self-deception is how we struggle to defend ourselves against such criticism. Typically, we feel resolute in justifying ourselves; especially when we perceive ourselves as misunderstood or misjudged, we can feel almost *obliged* to defend ourselves, highlighting our accomplishments and dismissing our critics.

For mindful leaders, such an exercise in defending ourselves against criticism and in turn seeking praise and confirmation is how we potentially blind ourselves as leaders and lose touch with our own sense of humor and confidence. Of course, this is not to say that accountability, recognition, and feedback are not vital at work. Recognizing a job well done and questioning errors is sound management. Rather, as mindful leaders, we do not confuse "praise and blame" with "success and failure": we know that those who succeed are often criticized and those who fail are often praised. We fully appreciate such ironies—often with a sense of humor. In fact, traditionally, it is said that mature and realistic leaders give praise to others and shoulder criticism themselves—a particularly skillful way to inspire the best in others.

I learned this lesson about praise and blame from my teacher during Buddhist seminary in a way that continues to cheer me up to this very day.

When I arrived at the seminary with about three hundred other Buddhist practitioners, we were all assigned rooms, given study materials, and signed up for certain work duties. The first days at the seminary were like arriving at college, filled with administrative chaos and a sense of new possibilities. We were told upon our arrival that our teacher, Chögyam Trungpa Rinpoche, who was leading the seminary, would be addressing us in the evening after dinner and that everyone was required to attend his introductory remarks. And it was with great anticipation that we all arrived that evening to receive Rinpoche and listen to his opening lecture. For the most part, Rinpoche reviewed the importance of working hard at our studies and respecting our fortunate circumstances. He reminded us that meditation practice was central and arriving on time at the shrine room was a must. He also made it a point to remind us that our rooms were to be kept neat and clean. He placed great emphasis on this, outlining the importance of offering an environment to ourselves and others that was uplifting and reflective of a disciplined mind. Having our rooms neat and clean was such a priority for Rinpoche that he informed us he would be traveling around the seminary and inspecting our rooms personally, so he expected us to follow through and not hide out in some kind of sloppy cocoon.

Of course, when I got back to my room, I made sure to put everything in its place: bed made, closets orderly, bathroom immaculate. I even arranged my shrine materials next to my bed to give a glow of reverence. I was well prepared for Rinpoche's visit, and I knew that he would see what a fine student I was.

Days passed, and one Sunday afternoon, rumors were that Rinpoche would be making his rounds. Having completed my duties and of course having an utterly spotless room, I decided to pay a visit to my good friend Boris, who was attending the seminary as well. I found his room on a lower floor, knocked, and entered as he swung the door open. I was immediately appalled.

My friend was frantically searching through his luggage for a particular item, and he had tossed the contents onto the floor and across the bed. Laundry, bathroom items, muddy boots, suits, and ties were everywhere. Being a carpenter and handyman, Boris had many tools large and small—all of which were scattered throughout the room. To make matters worse, his Buddhist texts and practice materials had slipped off a top shelf and were strewn among his tools. I laughed to myself and said, "Hey, Boris, this is a total mess, and Rinpoche is on the prowl. I would hate to be in your shoes if Rinpoche shows up! This is exactly what he warned us against doing."

"I know, I know," my friend said, panic-stricken, as he scooped up clothing and tools and starting stuffing them into the closet.

"Well, good luck, Boris. I'll see you downstairs for dinner later," I said as I turned to leave. I could hear him scrambling to create even a small sense of order.

As I approached the door, I thought to myself how fortunate I was that I had cleaned my room and was not in Boris's position. It was not my problem, I concluded, it was Boris's—and I opened the door to leave.

The second the door swung open, as circumstances would have it, I came face-to-face with Rinpoche's main attendant. A very amiable fellow with a great sense of humor, he was known throughout the seminary as a close student of Rinpoche's who traveled with him always. Although I was initially quite delighted to see him, he paused, looked at me, peered around into Boris's disastrous room, and said over his shoulder with a wry smile, "Rinpoche, you will want to see *this* gentleman's room."

As the circumstances started to dawn on me, I distinctly remember my mouth beginning to drop open. And, as the attendant moved aside, Rinpoche stepped up into the doorway and gazed over his glasses and straight into my eyes. For a brief moment, there was only silence, followed by the distinct sound of Boris hurriedly cramming his six-foot five-inch frame into his messy closet. As I heard him pull the door shut, Rinpoche gazed past me and got a clear view of the sloppy chaos that was supposed to be my room. He did not enter but simply looked for what seemed like an eternity.

Finally, he raised his gaze once again, looked directly into my eyes, paused, turned, and slowly walked away. The last thing I saw was the backs of both Rinpoche and his attendant, who was dutifully shaking his head in bewildered disappointment.

Needless to say, I was shocked. I was a victim of circumstances. While my room was spick-and-span, while my closets were clean and orderly, while my texts and practice materials were arranged with a glow of reverence, I was being held responsible—literally, personally responsible—for someone else's mess!! At the time, I was outraged, embarrassed, and shocked. I wanted to run down the hall and tell Rinpoche that I was not responsible—that I was a good little boy and that Boris was hiding in the closet. But that would have been even more pathetic than just standing there with my mouth open.

Throughout seminary, I struggled with the thought that Rinpoche probably saw me as a knucklehead rather than the deserving, disciplined student I so wanted to be. But over time—over many, many years— I came to understand this embarrassing moment as a great gift given to me by a master teacher.

No matter what, all of us at times will find ourselves standing in that doorway being held responsible for something not of our making. Maybe sometimes the room is clean and we are praised—but more likely, the room's a mess and we are blamed. Either way, to some degree, we are all at the whim of life's shifts and turns. It is simply a fact of life that circumstances will conspire to place on our shoulders problems, messes, and at times tragedies that are not of our making and often the result of someone else's poor judgment.

We can keep our desk clean and our job in order, we can build a life that has a glow of reverence—and out of nowhere, reality will drop an unwanted and undeserved burden in our lap. And it is right at this point that mindful leadership is required. Rather than feeling victimized; rather than deceiving ourselves with defenses and justifications, telling everyone that "Boris is hiding in the closet"; rather than cataloging the unfairness of it all over and over again, as mindful leaders, we are prepared to be utterly realistic—which presents us with a powerful and humbling challenge:

Do we have the courage to lay down our mistrust and anger and stop defending ourselves? Particularly when we feel utterly justified, can we be humble enough to shoulder the burden and give the praise to others?

Such is the challenge of the mindful leader.

Again, this does not mean that we should treat work's missteps as a comedy skit or avoid holding ourselves and others accountable. The Borises of the world are definitely responsible for cleaning their own rooms. Nor does it mean that we should not learn from criticism or listen to others. Rather, the problem lies in feeling threatened by work's ironies and then deceiving ourselves with all kinds of defenses, seeking praise for our glow of reverence and heaping blame onto others. By relating to work's difficulties—indeed, all of life's challenges—with the aim of avoiding blame and instead gathering praise, we end up with a scorecard instead of reality, and in the tradition of the mindful leader, such an approach to work and life is considered a coward's game.

Dropping the "scorecard" mentality does not alleviate the pain of being misjudged, however. It hurts to be mistreated and get the short end of the stick—especially when it's due to another's incompetence or arrogance or greed. But despite the discomfort, we can appreciate the irony of standing in the doorway—maybe even have a good laugh. As mindful leaders, we need not throw tantrums or assure everyone that we are good boys and girls. We need not chase the false hope of advertising that our job is nice and clean with a perfect glow of reverence. Because we know that work's doorways are filled with blunders and misperceptions, we can confidently relax and step beyond our personal disappointments with a sense of humor.

While I never had the opportunity to discuss this doorway mishap with my teacher, he nonetheless regularly spoke of the importance of taking the blame, suggesting, below, how we "bureaucrats" can be more skillful at work:

> That's a tip for bureaucrats. If individuals can take the blame themselves and let their friends off to continue their work or duty, that will make the whole organization work better and allow it to be much more functional. When you say, "You're full of shit! I didn't do such a thing. It wasn't me; it's you who did it. There's no blame on me," the whole thing gets very complicated. You begin to find this little plop of a dirty thing bouncing around in the bureaucracy, something like a football bouncing back and forth. And if you fight over it too much, you have tremendous difficulty dissolving or resolving that particular block, plop, slug. So the earlier you take the blame, the better. And although it is not really fundamentally your fault at all, you should take it as if it's yours. . . . Once you begin to do that it is the highest and most powerful form of logic, the most powerful incantation you can make.[1]

We all find ourselves in a world that demands us to take responsibility when we feel others should step forward first—whether it's a blossoming teenage son, a well-intentioned but arrogant boss, an incompetent politician, or just a messy roommate. Mindful leadership requires us to do just that—step forward first and take the responsibility with no complaint and no scorecard. Such humor and natural grace invite the best from others and create a workplace that is truly inspiring.

3. THE RED CAPE AND A MAD BULL
THE ILLUSION OF SECURITY

At times, it may seem quite reasonable to be wary at work, protecting ourselves from our jobs, colleagues, and employers. Our workplace can sometimes appear quite toxic with all its abuse, stress, and pressures, and protecting ourselves from such things seems to make sense in so many ways. Yet closing ourselves off from work may not be as reasonable as we think; in fact, it may be the very source of all our troubles. For mindful leaders, protecting ourselves from work reveals a shocking irony that is best illustrated by a brief metaphor that has been a favorite of mine for many years:

> Imagine for a moment that you are standing naked in the middle of a vast open field. It is a summer day, and the sun is shining and a cool breeze occasionally stirs the air. In your hand, you hold a bright red cape. Substantial yet flowing, the cape seems to fit easily into your palm, and it moves simply and elegantly. Directly in front of you, about seventy feet out, stands a large black-and-white bull. Some twelve hundred pounds of youthful muscle and power, the bull is clearly angry and is sharply focused on you.
>
> As the bull charges, you hold the cape up, and sure enough, you are able to avoid being gored by the bull's wildly jerking horns. Once again, the bull charges, and again, you use the cape to dodge and hide. Sometimes, the bull rests with a wary eye on you; other times, he circles and attacks. Sometimes, his power and weight knock you down or shove you rudely aside. Other times, he

simply stares. There is no one but you and the bull in a vast open field, and the only item you have is a red cape.

This distressing picture is a simple metaphor that may reflect for many of us how we occasionally feel at work. Our demanding careers, impossible job responsibilities, confused office relationships, unreasonable work hours, and hectic deadlines can often appear like an unruly, threatening beast that can attack and harm us at any given moment. And rather than opening to such difficult circumstances, we become wary, on guard, and self-protective, holding on to our routines, paychecks, job credentials, and territory for dear life. Work becomes an enemy rather than a friend, a threat rather than an invitation, a tiresome burden rather than a creative challenge, and at times, we find ourselves feeling under attack with very little protection.

This upsetting picture of the workplace as an unruly beast attacking us while we stand naked clutching a piece of cloth would be deeply disheartening, indeed, were it not for a profound irony: *the red cape, which seems to be protecting us from the bull, is in fact provoking his attack.* And the more we wave our cape in hopes of keeping ourselves safe and secure, the more we are actually provoking the bull to charge. In short, the more we try to protect ourselves from work, the more work seems to spiral out of control.

For mindful leaders, such irony demands the unthinkable—that we take a simple first step that appears utterly unreasonable:

Can we drop our cape? Can we stop protecting ourselves from work's raging pressures and instead lower our defenses and stand naked, fully open? Can we drop our desire to be safe at work and instead trust that we can engage our jobs confidently and authentically with no pretense or insecurity?

Such openness is the key to being a mindful leader rather than a wary and self-protective bystander. Too often, we find ourselves acting defensively at work—defending our prestige, our views, and our territory. At times, it seems that we have so much to lose: our financial security, our sense of accomplishment—even our identity. For mindful leaders, trying to protect such things is to fight a losing battle, for in doing so, we inevitably find ourselves insulting the world around us. Either through arrogance, fear, impatience, or just plain ignorance, we end up mistreating our world when we try to protect ourselves. We become fascinated with *our* job title, *our* promotion, *our* authority, which blinds us to our world; we place ourselves front and center and relegate everything and everyone else to the background, which provokes resentment, misunderstanding, and fear. Traditionally, this circle of protection and insult, in which we try to defend ourselves from the bull only to provoke him further, is considered the source of all human suffering. By putting ourselves first—by trying to make sure we are safe and sound—we inevitably shortchange our world, which is in need of inspiration, not games of hide-and-seek.

In order for us to tame the chaos at work, we must drop the cape that is provoking it, and in so doing, we must open: let go of our preconceptions and "great ideas"; drop our fear, hypocrisy, and arrogance and engage the situation from a fresh perspective with no defenses—fully naked. As mindful leaders, we are expected to step into our exposure rather than cover up—trust our instincts and intelligence rather than dodge life's circumstances. Such openness can at times appear utterly unreasonable, and for mindful leaders, such irony is a fantastic challenge. We can stop trying to protect ourselves from work, stop seeking security and comfort, stop holding on to credentials and prestige—simply drop the entire pretense of "being somebody at work" and stand naked as who we are, which may prove to be an enormously wise and liberating gesture, indeed.

4. ROSCOE THE CAT
BREAKING OUT OF STALE ROUTINES

Work has its rewards and delights: friendly colleagues, thriving commerce, challenging puzzles, and financial success. And to a great degree, we all go to work wishing such things for ourselves and others. Yet work seems to have a peculiar way of draining such delight from our lives, and instead we often find ourselves out of balance, carrying far more burden than reward. Over time, such burden can sap our enthusiasm: rather than being inspired to seek greater creative possibilities, we settle for predictable, possibly even stale, routine. Yet losing our enthusiasm for work may be less a function of the job than of how we choose to face the challenge. For the mindful leader, choosing predictable routine over creative instinct reveals a languid irony that is best illustrated by a brief story about a cat named Roscoe who was my New York roommate for more than ten years.

In the midst of my business career, personal circumstances necessitated that I find a new place to live in

New York, and with the help of some friends, I met a most gentle and kind man, Ken, who invited me to share his spacious apartment with large rooms and a view of the Hudson River. I settled into my new circumstances nicely. An added pleasure was the arrival of a black kitten named Roscoe, which Ken had adopted from a neighbor. Like all kittens, Roscoe endlessly entertained himself—chasing balls, jumping off furniture, springing out from behind closet doors. And, like most New York cats, Roscoe became unusually alert whenever the apartment door opened, for it was then that he would try to make his escape.

For the first several months after Roscoe's arrival, entering and leaving the apartment required a wary eye, for Roscoe was ever alert—ready to dash through even the slightest crack in the door. And when he did escape, he was apt to go on an adventure floor to floor, up and down stairwells, exploring garbage chutes, and on occasion a neighbor's apartment. I became quite familiar with Ken's constant refrain: "Watch out for Roscoe—don't let him get out!"

Roscoe had our sympathies, of course. All he really wanted to do was be a cat—roam freely, explore the unknown, maybe be really catlike and catch a mouse or two. So while Roscoe was a great kitten roommate, both Ken and I knew that, to him, the apartment was also a prison—a box that prevented him from being who he truly was. And, despite our protests and corralling, we secretly admired Roscoe's attempts at escape, and we secretly wished him well when he was able to orchestrate a breakout.

As Roscoe grew older, however, his attempts at escape took an ironic turn: whenever the door opened, rather than trying to break out to adventure, he instead became wary and afraid. There was nothing that Ken and I could point to that seemed to instill this fear in Roscoe—no dog attacks or nasty kicking kids. It just appeared that as Roscoe grew older, he became less adventurous, more inclined to stay within his "prison" than to escape. In fact, Roscoe grew fat, nibbling endlessly at stale bits of dried food, making halfhearted leaps at pigeons as they careened past his window, and occasionally wrestling a roach into submission as prey. For Ken and me, of course, not having to chase after our cat made life a bit more convenient, but for Roscoe, the change meant he was living a peculiar irony: an apartment in New York that had once been a prison restricting Roscoe's ability to be a cat had now become a security blanket. Rather than exploring the unknown, he had settled for the predictable; rather than catching a mouse or two, he nibbled at bits of dry kibbles; rather than hunting like a cat, he swatted at shadows and insects. Somehow, Roscoe's prison had become a drab palace, and his instinctive yearning for the unknown had become fear.

This brief story about my friend Roscoe the cat illustrates some of the irony we may experience when it comes to trusting our natural intelligence and instincts at work. We may have begun our careers trusting ourselves—eager to jump into the unknowns of the marketplace and unwilling to take "just any job." Maybe we went to New York or Los Angeles to become an actor or completed our MBA in order to start an innovative business and get rich. Or maybe we had ambitions to become a first-rate medical researcher seeking the cure for arthritis or a police officer wanting to bring order and justice to a difficult world. And, like Roscoe, when doors opened, we instinctively took the opportunity—trusting our natural resourcefulness—curious and willing to face the uncertainties. For many of us, our natural intelligence guided us to avoid the imprisonment of stale routines and tedious demands; we wanted creative challenge and discovery. And just as Roscoe wanted to be fully a cat, we too wanted to be fully human in our work.

Yet, somehow, for far too many of us, our instinctive yearning for creative challenge gradually transformed to the point where we ended up preferring security rather than fresh uncertainty, assurances rather than adventure, a reliable and stable job rather than an inspiring mission. And, like Roscoe, we may find ourselves at times chewing on dried, stale tidbits rather than savoring a tasty slice of life. Somehow, many of us have become imprisoned by our work, often fearing criticism, failure, or loss of income. And as long as the door doesn't open—as long as nothing threatens or intrudes on our stable job, we are willing to become a little bit like Roscoe: content to watch life from a comfortable window, snacking occasionally on predictable tidbits and avoiding adventures of all kinds.

For mindful leaders, then, Roscoe's circumstances present us with a basic question of trust:

> Can we trust that we are resourceful enough to explore life's uncertainties with confidence, clarity, and adventure? Can we reclaim our natural sense of enthusiasm

and abandon the prison of our fears and our need for a stable, secure job? Can we permit ourselves to be fully human?

This is not to say, of course, that we should be frivolous about our careers, preferring reckless adventure to reliable employment. Nor is my story about Roscoe meant to suggest that we permit chaos to waltz through our front door as it sees fit. Rather, the irony of Roscoe the cat reminds us that, as mindful leaders, we need to trust our basic intelligence—to have the confidence that comes from our own enthusiasm and delight and, at times, confront head-on how we imprison ourselves at work. For if we intend to lead and inspire the best in others, we must first trust the very best in ourselves—permitting ourselves to be fully who we are—permitting ourselves to be fully human.

3

THE ART OF SITTING STILL: MINDFULNESS MEDITATION

I N T H E T R A D I T I O N of the mindful leader, rather than leading with will, power, and ambition, we lead and inspire one another with openness, intelligence, and vulnerability. Such leadership is how we step beyond cowardice and self-deception and make a genuine contribution to our world, and traditionally, we develop such open leadership through mindfulness meditation.

Essentially, mindfulness meditation is a friendly gesture toward ourselves in which we take time to sit still—maybe for fifteen minutes, half an hour, or longer. We take a certain posture—sitting upright, relaxed, and alert. Our eyes are open, with a soft, relaxed gaze; our hands are placed palms down, gently resting on our thighs. Our chin is tucked in, and our gaze is slightly downward. Our face and jaw are relaxed, and our mouth is slightly open. We breathe normally and sit still. It is very simple—just sitting still and *being*. There is further instruction, of course, and it is best to receive ongoing guidance from someone trained and authorized to do so. For a preliminary review of mindfulness meditation instruction, see page 195 or visit my website, at www.awakeatwork.net.

Now, for many of us, the prospect of sitting still for thirty minutes or more a day in order to become a more effective leader may seem downright ridiculous. We have so much work to do, so much to accomplish, that to envision ourselves sitting still in a yoga studio or in our bedroom may seem like a colossal waste of time. Yet what appears to be a waste of time may actually be exactly what we are looking for.

As an organizational consultant, I have been asked many times to teach mindfulness meditation at business gatherings, and such sessions typically unfold along similar lines. After a few brief remarks explaining what mindfulness is and how it can impact our workplace, I give the meditation instructions, and as a group, we sit still for about ten to fifteen minutes. I am always fascinated by the initial silence of dozens of busy professionals who have stopped in order to be still. It's as if everyone in the room notices that a very simple yet vivid fact of life has been rediscovered. And, for the most part, people engage the silence sincerely, and during these brief sessions, they put genuine effort into following the instructions.

After a short time, however, some people begin to get visibly uncomfortable. Some stop following the instructions; others glance at their watches. Some even begin to read their newspapers. Eventually, the session ends, and I ask, "So, how did that go for everyone? Any observations about this practice of mindfulness meditation?" Inevitably, someone's hand shoots up, and he or she says, "I can't stop talking to myself. I just keep jabbering away, and my mind seems all over the place! I can't believe what I'm saying to myself!"

And it is at this very point, when we touch the restlessness of our mind, that we may glimpse why it is so important for us as leaders to practice mindfulness meditation. When we sit down quietly for a moment, we will notice, if we pay attention, that we don't want to be *where we are*. For whatever reason, we come to the conclusion that our experience in the present moment is not good enough, and we struggle to step away—possibly even *run away*—from being right here, right now. We want to be somewhere else—write a report, watch TV, or eat scrambled eggs. And often, we want to be someone else when we get there—skinnier, smarter, wealthier. When we sit still for a moment and notice this anxious struggle to get somewhere else, we experience firsthand how we shut down and *close off* from our world. We talk to ourselves, become impatient, possibly even panic or resent having to simply sit still for a moment. Such restless anxiety may seem like a simple nuisance—a distraction—an intrusion. For mindful leaders, however, our restless inability to be with ourselves is of the utmost importance, because such anxiety is how we close off from the facts of life, distort our sense of purpose, and miss the opportunity to appreciate our world. Such anxiousness is how we avoid being open.

Now, we may say to ourselves, "Well, yeah, I feel a bit anxious when I have to sit still for fifteen minutes. But wouldn't anybody? It's so boring. There is so much to do that anybody in their right mind would get anxious sitting around wasting time." On the surface, such sentiments may seem reasonable. But if we stick with our mindfulness meditation, we will eventually discover that we are not wasting time at all; in fact, by simply sitting still, we discover that we are *opening* to our lives in the present moment. And the anxiety we feel is not some annoying inconvenience but a basic "bewilderment" that keeps us stressed, impatient, and closed off throughout our entire lives. If we carefully examine our anxious impulse, it becomes apparent just how much time we spend closed off and out of touch during our day. Mindfulness meditation reveals many things, but first and foremost, it reveals in very stark and immediate terms our unease about being open and comfortable with ourselves.

Ironically, by simply sitting still, we commit to ourselves. We commit to opening rather than closing, being rather than achieving, engaging rather than rehearsing. It's like going to a "spiritual gym" for a leadership workout. Instead of lifting weights to strengthen our biceps or running on a treadmill to improve our cardiovascular system, we *let go* of the weight of our discursive anxiety and exercise the muscle of *being*—very directly, very authentically, and often very monotonously. By letting go and opening in mindfulness over and over again for an entire lifetime, we gradually develop the spiritual muscles of a mindful leader.

THE EFFORT OF "NONACHIEVEMENT"

There are two basic approaches we can take to cultivating our leadership talents through mindfulness meditation. One approach is to engage the practice as a method that allows us to improve ourselves. From this point of view, we can develop all kinds of fantastic abilities and reap many benefits. Recent scientific research, for example, seems to document that meditation produces a wide range of positive results: enhanced physical and emotional health, reduced anxiety and stress, feelings of joy and compassion, and much more.[1] And the Buddhist tradition speaks of the possibility of "enlightenment"—a final human fulfillment marked by wisdom, compassion, and bliss. But if we regard meditation solely as a technique for achieving all kinds of positive outcomes, we are likely to misunderstand what we are doing and possibly even confuse ourselves further. So, in order to avoid such a misstep, it is vital that we understand and embrace another approach to meditation, which focuses less on achieving results and more on *appreciating our experience as we meditate.*

When we approach meditation from the standpoint of appreciating our experience, meditation is no longer a method for achieving anything at all. Instead, meditation becomes an *expression* of who we are *as we meditate.* Understanding this distinction between trying to improve ourselves versus expressing who we are is central if we wish to cultivate the talents of the mindful leader. As mindful leaders, we are not trying to become more open; instead, we are interested in acknowledging that we are already open. We are not interested in becoming more wise or compassionate; we are interested in acknowledging the wisdom and kindness that we already embody. In short, as mindful leaders, we are not interested in improving ourselves or becoming happier; rather, we are interested in *being* who we already are—we are interested in discovering our basic sanity.

Now, to some, this may sound tremendously arrogant. "I don't need to improve myself because I'm perfect already. All I have to do is wake up to my inherent perfection, and everything will be just fine." Such an approach sounds like something straight out of the sixties flower-child movement— giving ourselves permission to roll around naked in open fields and neglect to pay the bills. But, of course, this is not what we are talking about at all. Rather, in mindfulness meditation, we are working to perfect what is traditionally called the effort of "nonachievement," in which we finally become comfortable with who we are rather than anxiously trying to become someone else. It is a profound sense of ultimate honesty in which we are willing to finally rest with whatever we are experiencing, and such ease is the very foundation of genuine leadership. Shunryu Suzuki Roshi, the famed Zen master, offers pithy advice on this point about meditating: "Try not to achieve anything special. You already have everything in your own pure quality. If you understand this ultimate fact, there is no fear."[2]

PART TWO

THE TEN TALENTS
OF A MINDFUL LEADER

IN ORDER to cultivate the talents of the mindful leader, then, we must practice mindfulness meditation with nonachievement in mind. But this is not to say that we do not experience results from our practice. For thousands of years, millions of people have practiced mindfulness meditation and experienced many positive outcomes, and as noted earlier, science is documenting more and more benefits every day. So we could quite reasonably ask, "How is it that we are supposed to cultivate leadership talents by sitting still and achieving nothing?"

Let's try a two-part experiment. First, put down this book and hold your hand in front of your face. Simply observe your hand for about thirty seconds. Now, if we were asked to describe this experience, most of us would say that we were just looking at our hand, not "achieving" anything. We don't "achieve" our hand; we don't achieve our foot or eye color or kneecap, either, for that matter. We *are* our hand and foot and eye color and kneecap. Now for part two of the experiment.

Hold your hand in front of your face once again, but this

time, flex your fingers open and shut, forming a fist and then releasing it. Observe this ordinary gesture a few times. Now, if we were to describe this experience, most of us would say that we were opening and shutting our hand—pretty straightforward. Yet there is much that we take for granted in making this gesture. In order to flex our hand, 27 bones, 29 joints, 123 ligaments, 34 muscles, 48 nerves, and 30 arteries coordinate into a seamless gesture that is profoundly elegant. Flexing our hand involves a series of activities that are quite astounding but are seemingly invisible and therefore taken for granted. And while none of us speak about "achieving" our hand, we could better appreciate the inherent marvel involved in flexing it.

Similarly, when we practice mindfulness meditation, we are exercising a variety of "spiritual muscles" that, for the most part, seem invisible and have been taken for granted. Just as we cannot "achieve" our hand, nor can we "achieve" just sitting. But when we flex our fingers back and forth to clench and unclench a fist, we gracefully *express* unseen forces, and in that same sense, when we practice mindfulness meditation, we equally express a variety of unseen, graceful, and profound *leadership* capabilities.

Over the next several chapters, we will examine these leadership capabilities and discuss ten gestures we make in meditation that we may be taking for granted—simple gestures such as breathing or sitting up straight that, when fully appreciated, express our inherent talents as a human being and a leader. We will explore how mindfulness meditation and "not achieving" exercise these unseen leadership muscles, and we will examine how we can exert such muscles at work—indeed, in all areas of our life—in order to make a helpful and inspiring contribution to our world.

4

SIMPLICITY

GETTING TO THE CUSHION

IN 1989, Richard Saul Wurman, award-winning architect and futurist, coined the phrase *information anxiety,* foretelling a crisis of frenetic insecurity that was quickly to become the hallmark of our twenty-first century. In a nutshell, information anxiety is what you and I experience when we are overloaded with data that adds little or no meaning to our lives. In his explanation of information anxiety, Wurman astutely defines some facts of life about our emerging information culture.

For example, read any weekday edition of the *New York Times* from cover to cover and you will have engaged more information than the average person would have come across in an entire lifetime in seventeenth-century England. In a sense, this fact of life is fantastic, good news. We are so fortunate to have such access—such a global view of our world. Yet Wurman also points out that unlike the *New York Times,* the typical newspaper read by the average American provides no global view and little access, since it contains only 13 percent news and *60 percent advertisements.*[1] Like so much other data we encounter, Wurman points out, most newspapers turn out to be "white noise," adding little or no meaning to our lives and serving only as a distraction—while, ironically, providing a blatant excuse to waste paper.

Now, for most of us, reading and disposing of the newspaper—whether it's the *New York Times* or the *Montana Red Nose Tattler*—is not a source of anxiety, but being relentlessly bombarded with massive amounts of information may be. Each day—via television, the Internet, e-mail, cell phones, radio, electronic billboards, and BlackBerry devices—we expose ourselves to hours upon hours of digital facts in our search for clarity and human connection. And our exposure to such gadgets starts early. About 40 percent of twelfth graders in the United States have more than four electronic devices in their bedrooms, feeding them continuous streams of data, entertainment, and, too often, mindless distraction.

Now, none of this is news to us. We live it each day. We all use our computers and watch our TV screens—we all listen to the radio and operate our cell phones and BlackBerry devices. Yet what may be news is the impact that such exposure is having on us—particularly at work. Studies have shown that thousands upon thousands of us each year are being diagnosed with ADT—attention deficit trait—a neurological disorder that perfectly fits Wurman's predictions about our growing information anxiety. The symptoms of ADT on the job are feelings of inner frenzy, impatience, and distractibility, all of which can undermine our best efforts to do our jobs and inspire others. Unlike attention deficit disorder (ADD), which is genetically based, ADT is considered a result of our being exposed to endless streams of stressful tasksl and complex data, leaving us feeling overwhelmed and longing for balance and clarity.

We develop ADT gradually. It's as if we never even see it coming. Faced with workplace "fire drills" accompanied by volumes upon volumes of information, we withdraw into a kind of "active stupor," and gradually, our judgment and balance are hijacked by panic and anxiety. In the words of Dr. Edward M. Hallowell, psychiatrist and business consultant, "Facing a tidal wave of tasks, the executive becomes increasingly hurried, curt, peremptory and unfocused, while pretending that everything is fine."[2] In the end, our ADT and information anxiety teach us to fake it—to camouflage our anxiety with false confidence, lacking any sense of humor or playfulness.

To a great degree, ADT can be seen as an expression of the unreasonable demands organizations sometimes place on us. Long hours, limited resources, unskilled managers, unseen competitive pressures—all can foster a work environment that is simply too much to handle. Of course, organizations have a responsibility to identify and resolve such dysfunction. Yet for us to succeed in a workplace inundated with meaningless data and frenzied tasks, we will need to unravel the source of this anxiety, which lies not in our workplace but within our own minds.

Experts offer much advice. "Anxiety-proof" the information you engage. Take a walk in the woods. Promote "positive emotions." Get some rest, eat well, and exercise. And at the core of all this advice is a very straightforward suggestion: *we need to simplify our lives.*

At first glance, cultivating simplicity in a world crowded with demands and endless pressures seems almost impossible. Yet, for the mindful leader, such simplicity is not as foreign as we may think and is in fact readily attainable.

GETTING TO THE CUSHION

In order to meditate, we must first actually "get to the cushion"—literally take time each day to stop and practice the art of sitting still. It's like saying, "If you want to be clean, you have to shower each day." Such a proposition seems quite reasonable and to the point. But ironically, when it comes to mindfulness meditation, we can experience tremendous resistance to actually *getting to the cushion.*

We have set up our meditation spot, maybe in our bedroom by the window or in a pleasant corner of our reading room. We have purchased meditation cushions in colors that match our decor. Maybe we have bought a little meditation bell that we can use to begin and end our meditation sessions. We have prepared well, and now it's time to actually sit down on the cushion—and we *plan* to do so each morning before work.

So we set our alarm a bit early—maybe for 6:00 A.M.—and sure enough, when it goes off, we remember, "It's time to sit." And we think, "Let me make my coffee first and then get to the cushion." Fine, that seems reasonable.

In the kitchen, as the coffee is brewing, we remember that we have to bring our clothes to the cleaner—we've been putting that off. In fact, we are not sure where we have left the sweater that we want to wear this weekend, so we quickly dash around trying to locate it. We think, "This will take only a minute, and then I'll grab my coffee and get to the cushion." Sure enough, as we search our laundry room for our sweater, we notice that our teenage son has once again dumped his gym clothes on the floor, and we decide to put them into the washer. It will take only a minute. Things seem to be going along smoothly as we begin to rush a bit more in order to get to the cushion, and sure enough, we find the sweater. Good news!

Back in the kitchen, we pour ourselves a cup of coffee, go to the refrigerator for some milk, and notice that our teenage son has emptied the carton—except for a few drops, of course —and has placed it back in the refrigerator in order to create the illusion that the family has milk for morning breakfast. As our blood pressure rises, we search for the Coffee-Mate, since morning coffee without milk is . . . well, it's not what we want. We locate the dairy substitute in the far reaches of our pantry, pour a bit into our cup, and we are off to the cushion, finally.

But, wait, along the way, we see our newspaper opened to the article that we want to copy for our team members at work, and we think, "I don't want to forget that. Let me put it in my briefcase downstairs." And we quickly do so. Back upstairs, we glance at the clock, and it's already 6:48. We think, "I've got to be in the shower in five minutes—I don't have time this morning to sit, but I'll definitely get to it tomorrow."

Such scenarios are not uncommon for those who practice mindfulness meditation. In an ironic kind of way, the difficulty of getting to the cushion starkly reveals our desire to be preoccupied—to have something to do—to keep busy. The closer we get to the cushion, the more we remember the e-mails that need to be answered, the laundry that needs to be washed, the newspaper that needs to be read. Through our struggles to get to the cushion, we discover that we are in fact resisting the simplicity of our lives.

For the mindful leader, then, getting to the cushion is how we cultivate the leadership talent of simplicity. When we literally sit down on the cushion, we stop our addiction to preoccupying ourselves. We gently set aside the distractibility and inner frenzy and express a willingness to experience the fresh immediacy of our lives. E-mails, laundry, shopping, TV shows, to-do lists—all for a brief moment are permitted to have their place, and we just sit down. Such a gesture is sheer simplicity. Absolutely nothing at all is required. Just sit down on a cushion—on the earth. By making such a straightforward gesture, we cut through our distractions and preoccupations and commit to simply being.

By doing such a thing repeatedly—by getting to the cushion day in and day out for the rest of our lives—we inevitably cultivate this vital talent of simplicity, which carries over into our everyday life and into our conduct as mindful leaders.

THE TALENT OF SIMPLICITY

There is so much at work that is not efficient: fun, the creative process, building consensus, solving problems, managing conflicts. Engaging these moments at work requires the talent of simplicity—the ability to slow down and appreciate what is going on—to give our work our resourcefulness and full attention. Yet work often does not seem to permit such simplicity, and this is why the frustrations of ADT and information anxiety are so powerful and distressing: *work demands that we slow down, but success demands that we hurry up.* We are being pulled in opposite directions—chasing after success while trying to attend to our lives.

We all want to do our jobs properly—to listen, appreciate, have fun, and build team spirit. But too often, success demands that we move along, get the work done, hurry up and meet the deadline. And instead of actually attending to what is needed, we too often "efficiently" speed past such human needs and subtleties. If we take an honest measure of what work requires, the speed and chaos of chasing success are more often than not just "white noise" distracting from us from getting the job done. As mindful leaders, the simplicity we cultivate on the cushion enables us to drop the frenzy of such distractions—to stop chasing the false hopes of success and instead appreciate our workplace and colleagues and do our jobs well. Instead of leaving us frantically intimidated by work's difficulties, simplicity reveals tremendous space and precision around such things— room for playfulness and creativity, room to listen and be deliberate. Just as with getting to the cushion, our simplicity on the job allows a "gap" to form in the tidal wave of e-mails, "fire drills," and workplace conflicts and permits some fresh air to circulate. Just as when we are sitting still on the cushion, we can be at ease with what arises and appreciate it. When we can create gaps of simplicity in our everyday experience, our obsession with "getting it right," grasping success, and avoiding failure no longer blinds us with anxiety. When we unfold the talent of simplicity on the job, workplace complications no longer loom as disproportionately alien and threatening but become "domesticated"—always a bit familiar and workable. When we exhibit the simplicity of the mindful leader, we create what is traditionally called *shamatha environment*—a peacefulness that inspires others to appreciate and learn from whatever occurs.

Creating peace at work may sound like some kind of naive idealism from the sixties, but in this case, it is not a far-fetched possibility. Such peace is not false harmony or wishful thinking. Rather, as mindful leaders, we tame our minds and offer others our sense of simplicity and precision. When we cultivate the art of sitting still, we discover that by simplifying our lives first, we can naturally help others do the same.

5

POISE
GATHERING THE MIND

NEGOTIATING is basic to everything we do at work. Whether we are scheduling meetings or establishing budgets, orchestrating a merger or closing a sale, all of us in one way or another negotiate. Throughout the workday, we are asked to make concessions, share resources, or maybe even give up a prized possession. Negotiating is how we manage workplace conflicts and ideally find common ground and agreement.

Typically, when we negotiate, we want to get what is best for ourselves. We want the best price for our home, the highest possible salary, and the corner office. We want a budget that meets all our needs and a sales territory that includes all the premium customers. It is quite natural to want the best for ourselves, yet negotiating from this mind-set can often spell disaster.

At Harvard Law School's Program on Negotiation (PON), practicing attorneys and law professors investigate some of the most intriguing aspects of negotiating, such as resolving conflicts among armed groups or advocating for the disadvantaged. During a PON conference entitled "Mindfulness in the

Law's ADR,"[1] several lawyers and professors discussed their published findings on the impact that mindfulness meditation has had on practicing attorneys, and the reports were quite encouraging. According to the presenters, lawyers who practice mindfulness meditation are inclined to have a greater tolerance for ambiguity, exhibit a higher level of self-esteem, seek and find creative solutions to difficult impasses, and empathize more fully with their clients. The presenters spoke of how mindfulness seems to strengthen ethical decision making and promote an improved atmosphere for joint problem solving. But most intriguing of all was the finding that mindful lawyers are inclined to step beyond "adversarial mind-sets."

Essentially, lawyers are driven by some basic negotiating rules; foremost among them is to maximize the position of their clients—even if it requires making unreasonable, misleading demands on others. For those of us such as myself who negotiate with lawyers in our daily work, such unreasonableness is unfortunately quite common. Verbose letters filled with inflated claims and false charges are the familiar calling card of many lawyers. And dialogue with attorneys is frequently marked by outrageous demands and hollow threats. Such is the lawyerly adversarial mind-set—a narrow and limiting viewpoint fraught with aggression and unhealthy impulses.

Of course, lawyers are not the only people caught up in such a charade. All of us in one way or another play such games. Bluster and half-truth, passive aggression, and outright bullying are all too common in workplace negotiations. But just like the mindful lawyer, the mindful leader is not trapped by such a mind-set because it lacks a basic understanding of how to be skillful at work. Such unreasonableness lacks poise.

GATHERING THE MIND

Once we get to the cushion, the very next gesture we make is to gather our minds, and we do so by taking a specific posture. We sit up straight with our knees loosely crossed. Our hands rest gently on our thighs with palms down, and our chin is tucked slightly in so as to straighten our neck. Our eyes are open with a soft gaze. By taking such a posture, we immediately become aware of our state of mind. Harried or calm, meandering or sharp, emotionally distraught or cheerfully present —our state of mind quickly becomes apparent, and in noticing such a thing, we gently and gradually gather our mind into the present moment. Such a gesture is the natural unfolding of simplicity. It's like taking a deep breath—a simple relaxing that pulls our experience back into a single point of nowness.

When we gather our mind in this way, we inevitably notice our surroundings: the morning light gently cascading through our bedroom window onto our worn, familiar closet door; the chirping sparrows fluttering among the branches of a backyard holly; the faint drone of traffic in the distance; the aroma of coffee brewing; the red pattern of a carpet. Gathering reveals that our mind is much fuller and larger than what we had "thought." The sharp vividness of our senses, the world around us, and our familiar "mind" all assemble as a singular moment, and it's at this point that we experience the talent of poise.

This poise is not based on stubbornness or stick-to-itiveness. It is not like walking a tightrope or balancing a stack of plates in one hand over our head. Rather, poise arises out of a basic discovery about ourselves—an insight that reveals larger possibilities. By practicing the art of sitting still, we discover, maybe for the first time in our lives, that *we are not the "voice in our heads,"* nor is our mind located between our ears. In fact, we begin to understand that life is not centered on "me" at all and that we have an opportunity to live our lives from a more relaxed and wider perspective.

Traditionally, the poise that is cultivated in mindfulness meditation is likened to the graceful self-assurance of a tiger. Ever watchful yet naturally at her ease, the tiger seeks no distraction or charade but is fully curious in the immediate moment. She need not make unreasonable demands on her world, since she is in command of herself. The tiger does not bluster or bluff or make hollow threats. She is not trapped by any adversarial mind-set, since she is utterly relaxed and resourceful. The tiger's senses are entirely alert, and she is completely willing. Whatever arises, the tiger engages with profound curiosity. The tiger never ornaments herself with extras in order to give herself false confidence. Her confidence is perfectly expressed by the ease of her natural poise.

In mindfulness meditation, we experience this ease of the tiger when we "synchronize"—when our body, mind, and world are gathered together and move seamlessly as one, which is the natural state of the mind. When we gather our mind into a single point of nowness, we discover that we synchronize into simplicity right here, right now. Such synchronized ease and powerful composure are the natural result of gathering our minds in mindfulness meditation and are how we carry the talent of poise into everyday life.

THE TALENT OF POISE

All of us at one point or another find ourselves trapped in mindsets at work. Maybe, like some attorneys, we get caught up in being adversarial. Or maybe we try to be a good boy or girl and follow directions in order to stay out of trouble. Or maybe we just think that work "sucks"—that it never offers us enough—and we feel put upon and a bit resentful. By gathering our mind in the art of sitting still, we begin to understand that we are not trapped in any of these mind-sets. We are not destined to be angry or jealous or frightened. Rather, by gathering our mind and "synchronizing" over and over again in meditation, we discover that we possess a natural comfort with ourselves comparable to that of a tiger. And, like the tiger, we are free—utterly free to be who we are.

Because, as mindful leaders, we are free, our poise is neither arrogant nor impoverished. Just as we have never seen a tiger running about announcing "Hey, look at me. I'm a tiger! I'm a successful, rich tiger that drives an expensive car!" neither do we need to announce who we are. Nor do we ever meet a tiger that apologizes for herself: "Gee, I'm sorry if my stripes are too bright. Would you like me to put on a sweater?" Our poise is self-contained and speaks for itself—no need to announce or apologize. Since mindful leaders are not entrapped by arrogance or impoverishment, we are comfortable with our authority, neither exaggerating nor shrinking from responsibilities. Like the tiger, the mindful leader confidently engages whatever arises.

Mindful leaders who have cultivated the talent of poise have enduring self-respect. Because our minds are gathered, we do not second-guess ourselves; we have an immediate appreciation of who and where we are and can therefore trust ourselves completely. This does not mean we don't make mistakes or occasionally take a wrong turn. The tiger is not infallible, but

she also does not fear political missteps or difficult circumstances. Rather, the talent of poise reveals that we can trust our
intelligence and basic humanity, and such dignified poise is
what the mindful leader offers to the workplace.

6

RESPECT
TOUCHING OUR HEARTS

ASK EMPLOYEES on any given day if they work for someone who is insulting and disrespectful, and one out of five will say yes. Essentially, millions and millions of us return home from work each day with feelings of having been ignored, disregarded, or possibly mistreated. Of course, such feelings of disrespect do not travel a one-way street. We can be sure that a good percentage of us who leave work feeling disrespected have actually directed such feelings at others—leaving our colleagues feeling dejected as well.

During my twenty-five years in corporate settings, I have found mutual respect among colleagues to be the single most important ingredient for building and sustaining healthy organizations. When we respect one another at work, we share a commonality that positively shapes just about everything: product reliability, workplace relationships, and public relations. Respect at work is not just about admiring another's competence or know-how. It is not about flattery or deference or "being nice." Genuine respect rests on a firm appreciation of our mutual humanity, and because of that, such respect is not easily broken and, when broken, is not easily repaired. When we respect one another's humanity, we acknowledge one another's deepest aspirations. We all want to raise a family or be part of one. We all want to be healthy and fulfilled, contribute to our world, and make life worthwhile. Colleagues and organizations can lose money, market share, and important deals, just as they can lose focus, perspective, or even confidence. But when we lose respect for one another, everything is put at risk.

In one of my assignments with a midsize scientific organization, I was asked to help out with a sizable layoff. Several dozen highly skilled scientists had been developing innovative medical products and devices for more than five years, and for all intents and purposes, their efforts had come to naught. In retrospect, people had a lot to be proud of. They had built a sophisticated and reliable experimental infrastructure, shaped a team of highly trained and competent professionals, and produced results using disciplined procedures. Unfortunately, their results were not coming fast enough, and their company had to be shut down.

As I met with many of these men and women, most spoke of a deep skepticism toward their managers. Employees felt, justifiably, that management had let them down, led them in the wrong direction, misread the marketplace, and chosen to develop the wrong products and devices. It was management that had failed to adapt its strategy fast enough, and now everyone would be out of a job. People felt dejected, sad, angry, bewildered, and more.

But the most intriguing and powerful view that many employees shared with me was that despite the widespread loss of confidence, they had not lost respect. In the end, employees still appreciated and felt "positively connected" with their leaders despite their lack of confidence in them. They understood that management did what it felt was best at the time. Despite the missteps, the employees knew that their management had always respected them as scientists and, most important, as human beings. The employees knew that management genuinely cared about their aspirations, families, and careers, and, in turn, the employees never lost such respect for their managers. While the employees were convinced that management had failed and no longer deserved their confidence, many felt that their managers deserved their respect.

Preserving such respect during difficult times is no small feat, for lawsuits, marketplace gossip, pilfering, and even sabotage can occur only in an atmosphere of disrespect. Employees are far less likely to take their frustrations out on organizations in which mutual respect is preserved. Unfortunately, I have witnessed countless examples of organizational disrespect toward employees, and the results were quite predictable. In this case, the management team and the displaced scientists went on to close their business with discipline and esprit de corps, and they all supported one another with a lot of heart during the difficult transition. Most employees quickly landed on their feet, and my sense is they left with few or no hard feelings.

Of course, respect in the workplace is vital regardless of whether the organization is going through difficult times or not. Whether our careers are moving forward or sideways— whether we are successful, failing, or somewhere in between— respect is the basic currency for building sane and healthy organizations, and for the mindful leader, such respect is an outgrowth of respecting ourselves on the cushion.

TOUCHING OUR HEARTS

Having taken our posture on the cushion and gathered ourselves, we inevitably notice that our mind displays a wide range of thoughts and emotions. Our mind can be calm and even like a clear running stream, or it can be swirling like a tornado. Sometimes it can be our best friend; other times, it can seem like our worst enemy. Meandering, rage-filled, sleepy, unruly, calm, worried, precise, or depressed: traditionally, experiencing such a range of feeling and texture to our mind while practicing mindfulness meditation is likened to taming a wild horse, and when we sit still, we come face-to-face with such raw power—and we gently touch it.

Normally, we like to pick and choose what we think and feel. We prefer joyful thoughts and stimulating emotions. We like to dwell on moments in our life that make us happy, and we savor feelings of thrilling passion and confidence. We also prefer to disregard our feelings of loneliness and jealousy and rage. They seem so unruly and messy and scary. Thoughts about irritating inconveniences such as paying the bills or dealing with a cranky boss—we try to weed those out of our lives. When we sit and practice mindfulness meditation, however, such weeding or sorting is impossible—we have no such luxury. We cannot pick and choose, focusing on pleasant emotions and sugarcoating or dismissing those that distress us. We actually welcome and respect all aspects of who we are. Whatever thoughts and emotions arise, we gently touch them—we literally acknowledge them. In meditation practice, we accomplish this by "labeling": when we notice our internal dialogue, we say to ourselves, "thinking." No thought or emotion is excluded. All are gently and respectfully touched with this simple gesture of labeling them "thinking."

Under normal circumstances, we tend to avoid touching our emotions—they are so rowdy and unmanageable. Rather than directly touch who we are, it's as if we would prefer to float around our home or workplace a few inches off the ground, gliding smoothly through our lives, perfectly at our ease—in great shape, successful, wealthy, and sought after. And when we can't float around our home or workplace, when our feet must actually touch the ground, we have to face the facts of life: *we are who we are.* We can't be selective, throwing out some bits and keeping others. When we come down to earth, we must touch our hearts and acknowledge who we are.

Unfortunately, when we come down to earth, we too often prefer to punish ourselves. Getting acquainted with the reality of who we are can be so raw and exposing that we prefer to find fault instead. "I never say the right thing, and nobody wants me." "I don't know how to dress, and my butt is too big." "Look at my hair—it's as crinkly and chaotic as my personality." When we treat ourselves as unworthy of being who we are, we show tremendous disrespect toward ourselves. When we try to pick and choose our feelings and thoughts, and try to float around a few inches off the ground as "perfect" people rather than keep our feet on the ground as who we are, we not only disrespect ourselves but also lose heart and inspiration for living our lives.

By touching our hearts in meditation, we stop disrespecting ourselves and show a willingness to embrace who we are —not just the good and happy parts but our apparent shortcomings and fears and anxieties as well. By sitting still and permitting ourselves to look at whatever arises—to actually touch and acknowledge it—we show the utmost respect for ourselves.

For mindful leaders, touching our unfolding hearts on the cushion is central because it teaches us to respect who we are and make friends with ourselves. Traditionally, such friendship is called *maitri,* which is a kind of warmth and kindness that we develop toward ourselves—a natural sense of health and well-being. By simply sitting still and acknowledging whatever arises, we naturally develop maitri: we make friends with ourselves. Maitri is our ability to touch our hearts and keep our feet on the earth as real, authentic people rather than trying to float above the ground as ideal people. By developing maitri on the cushion, mindful leaders naturally extend such heart and friendship to others. By learning self-respect in our practice, we naturally offer such respect to our world.

THE TALENT OF RESPECT

Extending the respect we learn on the cushion into the workplace is on one level quite ordinary and familiar. It is very similar to conventional day-to-day respect, such as not running stop signs and not stealing from shareholders. In this case, however, the mindful leader seeks to extend such respect as far as possible. It's exactly the opposite of the common cowardly attitude of "my way or the highway." The talent of respect shows us how to appreciate, understand, and work with what *is* instead of insisting or resisting at work.

Organizations have their procedures and habits and "unspoken rules," many of which seem strange, convoluted, and at times dysfunctional. For the mindful leader, such things are not to be resisted but "touched"—understood, appreciated, acknowledged. This is not to say that we must simply toe the line, follow orders, and rearrange the deck chairs on the *Titanic*. Quite the contrary. The talent of respect teaches us to fully appreciate our circumstances and acknowledge exactly what is going on. And if we find ourselves shouting orders from the deck of the *Titanic,* the talent of respect does not permit us to sugarcoat or turn a blind eye to such a reality.

When we extend the talent of respect to our colleagues at work, we appreciate the unique styles, skills, and struggles we all bring to the challenge. Rather than picking and choosing, we learn to recognize that all of us at work have our shortcomings and strengths. We are all a bit arrogant, fearful, and lost. While many of us try to hide such shortcomings and put on our game face, the reality is that all of us suffer at work, and for mindful leaders, this is not offensive or embarrassing but worthy of our respect and understanding. In the same way, we appreciate others' talents and abilities: the customer service rep who can solve just about any problem, the custodian who has been detail-oriented and vigilant for twenty years, the senior executive who stays late every night and always greets subordinates with a pleasant "hello," the sales manager who never loses enthusiasm. For mindful leaders, appreciating our colleagues' better qualities is never a chore. Learning to appreciate and respect ourselves on the cushion makes it easy to appreciate and respect others.

Traditionally, the talent of respect is said to introduce us to a profound insight called *ksana,* or "unique occasion." Essentially, by practicing the art of sitting still and cultivating the talent of respect, we discover the simple, penetrating fact that we have appeared on this earth, and when fully appreciated, such an insight is profoundly illuminating and humbling. Before we worry about paying the bills, before we celebrate another success or take another vacation, before we hurry on to something else, we can rest for just a few seconds and actually glimpse ksana: the profoundly unique occasion in which we find ourselves—right here, right now. For the mindful leader, such vast and profound appreciation is the very core of respect. Viscerally understanding the preciousness of our circumstances in the present moment is what teaches respect, and the mindful leader never ignores such teachings.

7

COURAGE
LETTING GO OF THOUGHTS

W HEN I STARTED my career on Wall Street in the early 1980s, I was struck by the caste system that dominated the halls of American capitalism. Of course, there was the typical pecking order of job titles, but what was most intriguing was not so much the corporate chain of command as an invisible wall between what were called the "back office" and the "front office."

Those in the front office—the bankers, traders, and brokers —made fabulous incomes selling stocks and bonds and financing corporate takeovers. They worked hard, played hard, and were celebrated as the heroes of Wall Street. Those in the back office—the neglected armies of operations clerks, accountants, and information technology professionals—worked for modest pay and processed the financial instruments, ensured compliance, and reconciled account balances. No detail was taken for granted in the back office when it came to keeping order in the bowels of capitalism.

The invisible wall between the back office and the front office was thick and high. There were the "heroes" in the front and the "grunts" in the back—those who "made it happen" and those who "watched it happen and then cleaned it up." The front was the place to be; the back was for wannabes. On Wall Street, everybody left the office late—some in limos, others on the subway. But an ironic twist to this rigid caste system was emerging in the 1980s—one that was to reveal the wannabes as the true heroes.

In the early 1980s, Wall Street remained a paper-intensive, control-oriented industry processing millions of tons of documents each year. But with the rapid development of data centers and real-time systems, financial instruments went digital, and the ability to process them quickly created a competitive edge. The front office could no longer succeed unless it was supported by systems and operations that could execute its trades better than the competitors. More than ever, time had become money, and the firms that had a crack back office became the preferred vendors. Transforming from a paper-intensive, control-oriented bureaucracy to a technology-driven service business became the number one priority for every Wall Street firm. Whichever firm succeeded first could then afford to buy its competitors, and the race was on.

Typically, the front office led the way—only now, armies of clerks and supervisors from Brooklyn, the Bronx, and Queens were expected to save the day, but few took the initiative and many resisted change. The innovative, fresh ideas were there, but lips were sealed.

In my capacity as vice president of human resources, I worked with management to overcome this silent resistance—a challenge that I quickly learned was common throughout the financial industry. The unwillingness to speak up, share ideas, and embrace technology was widespread, and it was the first time I had encountered such a cultural dysfunction. It got my attention, both professionally and spiritually: *how could thousands upon thousands of hardworking, dedicated, and intelligent men and women refuse to share opinions and embrace changes designed to improve their work?*

I interviewed hundreds, surveyed thousands. Over the years, I facilitated hundreds of focus groups and training sessions seeking the source of this collective reluctance to speak openly and embrace change. Time and again, exactly the same answer emerged: *people were just plain afraid.*

At the time, this answer seemed pretty obvious to most employees and managers. I can't count how many times I heard refrains such as "I could be fired for saying this!" or "We'll get in trouble if we try that," or "It's not worth the risk—I have a mortgage to pay and kids to send to college." But, for me, such widespread anxiety about speaking one's mind was astonishing.

Research has documented that this lack of courage in the workplace is as widespread and deeply entrenched today as it was on Wall Street in the eighties. Studies have shown that the majority of us are unwilling to address certain off-limits topics, such as our boss's behavior, distressing conflicts, poor decisions, or substandard coworker performance.[1] And organizations practice "ideacide"—a willingness to stifle creative initiatives and "kill" innovative ideas in order to preserve the status quo.[2] And perhaps most surprising is that more and more of us each day seem to accept that fear has become an accepted aspect of our modern work life.

For mindful leaders, however, such widespread fear at work—and indeed, in our lives—reflects a greater and more profound spiritual crisis. For when we look closely at our workplace fear—when we take the time to rest mindfully with our anxiety, hesitation, and distress—we discover that we are *holding back, holding in,* and *holding on.* Like so many of my colleagues on Wall Street, we, too, are trying to hold on to our jobs, prestige, and paychecks—holding back from speaking our minds. And in the end, we hold in and resist, often living stressful and burdensome lives. Traditionally, such holding on or grasping is considered the cause of losing our way in life and is how we can end up behaving like cowards. As mindful leaders, then, rather than holding in, we learn to *open out;* rather than holding on, we learn to *let go.*

LETTING GO OF THOUGHTS

By taking our posture on the cushion, gathering our minds, and sitting still, we commit to making friends with ourselves, and we develop maitri. Such warmth and respect toward ourselves are how we acknowledge our state of mind. Whatever arises when we sit—highly emotional thoughts or bland meanderings; cheerful, exciting feelings or distressing, panicky sensations—we respectfully acknowledge each experience by labeling it "thinking." By labeling our emotions in such a way, we are not trying to dismiss or repress them, nor are we trying to encourage or sanitize them. Rather, by permitting ourselves to see and experience our emotions clearly, allowing them to be as they are, we are actually respecting our emotions. By practicing the art of sitting still, we stop dressing our emotions up as forms of entertainment or pushing them into a closet out of laziness or fear. We make friends with ourselves by seeing clearly who we are and touching our hearts.

Once we acknowledge our emotions by labeling them "thinking," our next gesture is to *let go:* we release our grasp on our internal dialogue and gently bring our attention to our breath. We let go of our inner dramas and story lines and guide our attention to the simple yet vivid experience of breathing.

When we examine this gesture of letting go carefully, we will notice that we are exerting very subtle yet potent "effort"— exercising spiritual muscles, so to speak, that we may not have known we had. When we *let go* and bring our attention to our breath, we are also simultaneously *opening* and *leaping*. It is like jumping from a rock overhang into a favorite swimming hole. In order to do such a thing, we must first let go of our hesitation.

For most of us, standing on the edge of a diving board or rock overhang and pausing before we leap into a pool of water is a common experience. And we all know why we hesitate. We aren't sure we can leap safely; we recoil from the unknown. We are uncertain and want reassurance. In the end, then, such a pause requires courage—the courage to let go of our security, hesitation, and doubt and engage the unknown directly. And once we let go and commit to fearlessly jumping into the reality of a cold, refreshing pool, we must immediately *open*. It's like letting go of a hundred-dollar bill that we are holding between two fingers—as soon as we let go, we notice our hand is open.

And, finally, we *leap* into the present moment. And for those of us who have been fortunate enough to have jumped into a cold running river or an inviting pool of water, we know that moment of freedom and joy and uncertainty. In a split second, we are free and open and utterly on our own. While it may not be as exciting as diving into our favorite swimming hole, when we let go of our inner dialogue and plunge into the simple immediacy of our breath, we are also expressing a courage and confidence in ourselves that are unmistakable and fundamental to being mindful leaders.

When we look carefully, we will notice that it is uncomfortable to let go of a thought or an emotion when we practice mindfulness meditation. Our internal dialogue and emotional rehearsing provide a sense of personal safety and comfort. We want to savor our emotions, review nagging problems, speculate about possibilities. We want to linger with our internal dialogue—even if it's for just another second or two. On the surface, such activity seems quite ordinary. But when we practice mindfulness, we begin to recognize that the desire to hold on to our thoughts and emotions more often than not is simply insecure hesitation. Like the actor who would rather rehearse his lines than walk onstage and perform, our tendency to talk to ourselves is a desire to remain secure rather than *be*. Traditionally, such reluctance to step out from behind the curtain of our discursive mind is considered the very essence of cowardice, condemning us to live the life of a *tudro*. In Tibetan, *tu* means "hunched," and *dro* means walking—walking hunched over with our head down—the psychological posture of a coward.

Typically, we may associate courage with rescuing children from a burning house or speaking up and challenging a vicious dictator. No doubt, such brave gestures are inspiring acts of courage. In this case, however, we practice mindfulness in order to cultivate the very essence of courage—the courage to step out from behind our insecurity, stand up straight, and simply *be who we are*.

Now, that may not sound very reassuring to those trapped in a burning building. We can't say to those in need of our help, "Hey, I'm out here standing up straight and cultivating the courage to 'be me.' I'll let the firefighters do the rescuing—I'll just stay put and be who I am." But the courage we cultivate on the cushion is neither so naive nor so crass; rather, it is exactly what is required in our everyday life. In order for us to be truly brave, we must first and foremost step past our need for security, sacrifice our personal sense of comfort, and then do what is decent and right. All acts of courage—great and small—demand that we first let go of our personal need for security, and that is exactly what we, as mindful leaders, cultivate on the cushion.

For mindful leaders, then, the courage to express genuine bravery in our everyday life must start with letting go on the cushion. When we let go in meditation, we gradually learn that we no longer have to keep our heads down and protect ourselves from life; instead, we can stand up and live our lives straightforwardly. Such courage reveals that we need not argue with life's demands or assign blame. For mindful leaders, the hypocrisy and cowardice of keeping our heads down as tudros is confronted and unraveled first and foremost on the cushion, and it is from here that we can then extend such courage into our everyday life.

THE TALENT OF COURAGE

Extending the courage we cultivate on the cushion into the workplace is never as simple or dramatic as we might hope. We may think that if we have courage at work, we will be able to speak our mind whenever we want, confront conflicts head-on, and be decisive in difficult situations without looking back. Unfortunately, too many leaders see courage in such terms and end up bullying their way through workplace difficulties rather than expressing genuine fearlessness. The courage of mindful leaders is not an excuse for being impulsive or aggressive or politically tone-deaf. Rather, when we express the talent of courage on the job, it always begins with letting go—letting go of arrogance, rigidness, and small-mindedness of all kinds. Mindful leaders express courage by not holding on to fixed views, wielding credentials, or stubbornly insisting on a position. Clinging to our prestige, authority, opinion, or command is not a priority for mindful leaders, and when we let go of such fixations, we find that we are, as traditionally described, "suddenly free from fixed mind."

Such freedom does not mean that we are not firm in our convictions as leaders. In fact, the duplicity and arrogance we so often witness in some leaders frequently reflects a willingness to compromise a conviction in hopes of preserving prestige, wealth, or status. As mindful leaders, we in fact have the courage of our convictions, and because of that, we can let go of our fear and hesitation and pettiness and freely engage our workplace challenges.

Being courageous at work often requires us to confront difficult issues and shake up the status quo. Voicing our viewpoint and raising off-limit topics may be uncomfortable for us and others. But for mindful leaders, such discomfort is not unfamiliar territory because we have had the courage to address *our* difficult issues, shake up *our* status quo, and make friends with *our* off-limit topics *on the cushion*. And by doing so, we learn that expressing courage is not a matter of winning or losing or refusing to back down from a conflict. We learn, instead, that courage is about being emotionally comfortable with ourselves—letting go of anger, arrogance, prestige, greed —and being honest with ourselves right here, right now, on the spot.

Such honest, intelligent courage can be cultivated in organizations only at a very human level, and while on Wall Street, many of us did just that. Of course, we implemented training programs, instituted companywide climate surveys, and conducted employee feedback meetings. But in the end, what really inspired courage among the back office folk were the human moments with senior executives who truly had the courage to let go of their titles, prestige, and limos and roll up their sleeves, work side by side, and listen. In the end, what made the difference were power brokers willing to dive into unknown waters—to leave their corner offices, cross the invisible divide, and openly appreciate their back office colleagues. And it is at this utterly human level where we, as mindful leaders, can express the talent of courage.

8

CONFIDENCE
OPENING TO WHAT IS ARISING

No MATTER how hard we try to keep our jobs and careers on track, they just don't seem to cooperate—they constantly misbehave. One minute we are on our way to a promotion, and the next we are being transferred to Antarctica. Or maybe our boss has closed the largest sale in the history of the company and, as she basks in the glory, asks us to manage the account. We're enthused and ready for the challenge, but we find that she failed to bid it properly, and now we're accountable for a project that'll be lucky to break even. Such mishaps occur frequently, and we all know the score. The list of unruly possibilities is endless.

Typically—and understandably—we work really hard to avoid such difficulties at work. None of us wants to get promoted to a job that's going to be eliminated; no one wants to be shipped off to a desk in a snowy corner of Siberia. Yet facing workplace difficulties confidently and skillfully when they do eventually arise is vital, and for the mindful leader, such confidence demands openness.

In my role as a human resources executive, I have had to eliminate many jobs, displace many employees, and advise others that they must seek employment elsewhere. While it is the

least pleasant part of my job, it nonetheless requires much care
and skill. I recall once eliminating the job of a warehouse manager. The woman, Rose, was a longtime employee, had an
excellent track record, and was 100 percent reliable. Unfortunately, the warehouse she managed was being consolidated
with four other companies, and her services were no longer
needed. When I met with Rose to review her separation benefits and severance package, she was clearly distracted and
impatient. "Just read me the letter, please, and let me be on my
way," I recall her saying to me.

On the one hand, Rose was making my job easier. I, for one,
do not enjoy firing anyone, and the shorter such an experience, the better. Yet I could tell that Rose wanted to move on
from the conversation for a reason that was not clear. My gut
was telling me that something was missing, but I did not know
for sure what it was. I abandoned my rush to get through the
conversation and asked, "Rose, I know you want to get out of
here, and I appreciate that—but I can't help but feel that I'm
missing something. Can you help me here? What am I missing?" I knew that by being open to Rose in such a way, I could
be inviting any number of responses but was truly touched and
a bit overwhelmed by what she had to say.

"You're not missing anything," she quickly responded. "For
me, it's all very simple. For the past seventeen years, I have
been getting up every morning at 5:00 A.M., getting my para-
plegic son out of bed, dressing him, feeding him, and driving
him to the day-care facility, then arriving here at 6:30 sharp.
As you know, I run a tight ship until 5:30 every day. When I
leave here, I pick my son up, bring him home, bathe and feed
him, and read him a story before he goes to bed at 9:30. I have
been doing this now for seventeen years, and nothing in this

little letter is going to get in my way. So don't worry—you're not missing a thing."

I'm not sure what Rose saw that morning as she stood there giving me this speech, but what I saw was a tremendously brave and dignified woman. I felt so fortunate that I had taken the time to mindfully open up and be available to whatever might be happening rather than rushing past the discomfort. She had taught me a profoundly valuable lesson and inspired me to reexamine a critical but often overlooked aspect of employee layoffs—*families at risk.*

In formulating policy for this layoff, which included 250 other employees, I had forgotten to consider extending health benefits for employee families managing medical crises. Immediately after my meeting with Rose, I called headquarters and requested a quick confidential analysis on employees about to be laid off whose families were struggling with medical crises such as cancer or major surgery. And sure enough, we found a dozen others in circumstances similar to Rose's, and we extended to them an additional six months of health coverage in order to relieve them of the expense during their job search. Now, my meeting with Rose is a simple story, but it is what our work world is made of—simple moments in which being mindfully open and available to others can make all the difference in the world.

OPENING TO WHAT IS ARISING

When we sit and practice mindfulness meditation, we *open* to whatever arises over and over and over again—possibly millions of times if we choose to practice mindfulness for our lifetime. When we sit still on the cushion, we acknowledge our emotions and thoughts by labeling them "thinking," we let go of our internal dialogue, and then we open to our world—very simply, very directly.

When we examine this experience of opening, we find that we are expressing a part of ourselves that we may tend to overlook: *we trust ourselves completely*. In order to open, we must let go of our familiar thoughts and emotions—we must step out from behind the safe curtain of our inner rehearsals and onto the stage of reality—even if it's for just a brief moment. When we open on the cushion, we renounce our attachment to our emotional security blankets over and over again. We drop our pretense and story lines and stand naked. Maybe we would like to protect ourselves; maybe we would like to stay behind the curtain and rehearse our lines—but we have the courage to *let go,* and such courage naturally blossoms into the confidence to be fully open.

Now, of course, when we practice mindfulness on the cushion and we open, we find that we are sitting still looking at the floor, which is not particularly dramatic. Our hands are placed gently on our thighs, our legs are loosely crossed, we are sitting up straight, and we are looking down at the floor, or if we are sitting with others, we may be resting our gaze on our neighbors' backs or the cushions on which they are sitting. When we engage our experience in meditation, we are confronted with the stark simplicity of our lives, which is showing up to be a most unexciting event, indeed. We are merely sitting still—just sitting. We cannot be selective. We can't fly around the room or distract ourselves with a crossword puzzle. We have no emotional life preservers, and no one is patting us on the shoulder to congratulate us for meditating so well. Of course, we may retreat back into the inner sanctum of our discursive minds to rehearse our lives one more time—just to make sure. But in that case, we once again acknowledge our emotions, let go, open, and we find ourselves right here—simply and uneventfully here. Such a gesture of being here on the cushion without picking and choosing, without entertainment, without any support whatsoever reveals that we trust ourselves—that we are intelligently confident in being who we are right now on the spot. And for mindful leaders, bringing such confidence to the workplace can inspire a sense of ease and reassurance for both ourselves and our colleagues.

THE TALENT OF CONFIDENCE

Extending the confidence we cultivate on the cushion into the workplace is about being open to whatever presents itself. Normally, we resist difficulties and welcome successes. We are willing to be open to pleasures and achievements of all kinds, but we want to ward off the inevitable unruliness of our lives. For mindful leaders, such picking and choosing is not only unnecessary, it is painful and cowardly. Trying to make our lives secure by amassing all the goodies and avoiding all the difficulties turns out to be an aggressive game devoid of courage and confidence in which we try to hold on to our lives rather than let go and live them fully. For mindful leaders, the openness and confidence we cultivate on the cushion overcomes this aggressive mind-set, permitting us to be available to our work—whether pleasant or distasteful, cheerful or disappointing. We don't rush through firing someone because we are uncomfortable; we don't throw a tantrum because our

BlackBerry is on the fritz and won't display our favorite icons. We don't ignore inconvenient business facts so that we can recklessly present an upbeat public relations picture. The confidence of mindful leaders introduces the possibility that we can be thoroughly realistic about our lives—receptive to anything and everything that occurs.

Of course, there are many distasteful experiences that we tend to resist at work—indeed, in our lives in general. But the art of sitting still teaches us that when we resist—when we hold on and tense up and hold in—we only make matters worse; and we do have a choice, because we know how to let go and open. For the mindful leader, letting go and opening to our workplace, with all its rewards, difficulties, and challenges, is the sane and confident thing to do—it puts us in contact with reality, and such contact is genuine, fresh, and raw. By opening to our experience, we cultivate the talent of confidence, and for mindful leaders, expressing such confidence is the key to inspiring a fearless, dignified, and joyful workplace.

9

ENTHUSIASM
LEAPING INTO UNCERTAINTY

MOST OF US can remember our first job. We may have packed grocery bags or pumped gas. Maybe we babysat for the neighbor's children or washed dishes. Whatever our memory serves up, we all started our life-long pursuit of livelihood somewhere at some time. And as with most events in our youth, there was probably something fresh about our first job—something enticing and bright.

I was twelve years old when I got my first job at the local grocery store. The fellow who hired me drove an orange car, wore his hair combed up in a bizarre pompadour, and was always pulling gags on regular customers. He hired me to do odd jobs—packing ice, unloading trucks, sweeping the floor—easy tasks that the owner didn't want to do, and I was delighted to take them on. I was excited to see results for my efforts, and I got to have a dollar in my pocket—a dollar that I'd earned. When I was a young boy, work was someplace where I could express my enthusiasm and cheerful delight.

Like most of us, I have held many jobs since then: truck driver, librarian, dishwasher, waiter, carpenter's assistant, road builder, tutor, educator, and corporate executive. Each had its challenge and its own way of being bright and enticing. Yet, as

I grew older, work began to lose its delightful appeal, and my enthusiasm slowly ebbed. Somewhere along the way, my experience of work shifted. When and where and how, it's hard to say. The attraction seemed to slip away imperceptibly. As responsibilities multiplied, the ground of livelihood shifted. What was once fresh and inviting became more predictable and tedious. What was once a free expression became an obligation. As work gradually became more a burden than a delight and my enthusiasm waned, I began to question: *What am I doing this for? Why am I working?*

For many of us, the answer seems obvious. We have bills to pay and obligations to meet; we want to send our children to college, pay our rent, and make a contribution. We work to solve problems of all kinds and keep some order in our lives. In the final analysis, most of us work *because we have to.* For mindful leaders, however, such obligation, while important, is not our primary purpose at work. Before we pay the bills and solve problems, before we shoulder another duty and make another contribution, we all want to enjoy ourselves at work. We want to engage our jobs—indeed, our entire lives—with the very same fresh delight that we discovered in our youth when we got our first job. In the end, we go to work out of obligation, but what we really want is to have fun.

Reclaiming such youthful enthusiasm is not just a romantic pursuit in which we conjure up notions of ideal employment. We need not leave our job as an engineer or a doctor so we can start an ant farm business or become a Zen *roshi*. For mindful leaders, reclaiming our vigor and enthusiasm at work is a very practical matter and comes from rediscovering exactly who and where we are.

LEAPING INTO UNCERTAINTY

When we examine how we practice mindfulness on the cushion, we notice that we are making a series of subtle and profoundly potent gestures that happen almost simultaneously. We *touch* our thoughts and emotions, *let go* of our grasp on our discursiveness, *open* to our experience, and then *leap* completely into the present moment. Such a series of gestures happens in an instant, yet each gesture has its own wisdom and vitality.

When we bring our attention from our thoughts to our breath in the present moment, we will notice that we do so suddenly: an abrupt shift occurs, like leaping. We cannot meander into the present moment. We can't say, "Hey, I think I'll be a little present—but not completely because I still want to rehearse my life." Such an approach is impossible. Either we are fully here or we are not. We cannot kid ourselves or pretend. Just as with leaping into our favorite swimming hole, it's all or nothing. As my teacher Chögyam Trungpa Rinpoche put it:

> You might wonder if you will sink or hurt yourself if you jump. You might. There is no insurance, but it is worthwhile jumping to find out what will happen. The student warrior has to jump. . . . Some kind of leap is necessary.[1]

The reason why such a gesture is so sudden has less to do with our leaping and more to do with what we are leaping into. Typically, we experience our lives as a running commentary. We are basically talking to ourselves—recalling what has happened and planning what needs to be done, evaluating our experiences and preparing for others. Traditionally, it is said that by living in such a mind-set, we are caught in what Tibetans call a *bardo*, or "in-between point" (*bar* means "in between," and *do* means "place"). The irony is that being caught in a bardo is like sitting in a waiting room or waiting in a sitting room and trying to determine what is going on. We are waiting "in between places": we are not fully engaged but sitting on the sidelines and waiting—thinking about life rather than living it. While we are waiting, however, life is going along perfectly as it is—unfolding on its own vivid, terrifying, and delightful terms. So, no matter how much we might want to wait in our bardo trying to figure out what is going on, reality is occurring with or without our full participation.

Each time we come back to our breath in the present moment, we decide to leave the waiting room and participate. We no longer linger in between places but actually commit to a place that is right here, right now. We notice that the only commitment we can make is to whatever is already happening. We can't invent it. We cannot author the present moment, since it is already fully unfolded in all its power and simplicity. Leaving the waiting room involves discovering that what we have been waiting for has been occurring all along. Reality didn't stop because we chose to wait in a sitting room and rehearse our lives. So, when we bring our attention to our breath and fully engage the present moment, we wake up to what has been going on all along. What we are leaping into arrives fully happening, which is the abruptness that we experience on the cushion when we leap.

But what are we actually leaping into? When we leave our waiting room and commit to the present moment, what is it that we commit to? Traditionally, the answer is that we are committing to *nothing*—or, more precisely, *sunyata,* which means "emptiness." On the one hand, this response is a bit too cute, and it makes sense to be suspicious of such a seemingly pat answer. However, by examining somewhat more closely, we can discover the very source of the youthful joy and enthusiasm we wish to reclaim.

Typically, when we think of *emptiness* or *nothing,* we may think of a large, black open space—bland, dark, and utterly uninteresting. But in this case, the emptiness to which we are committing is far from dull and boring. When we examine our routine everyday experience, we will notice that a lot is going on. We have friends and family whom we love; we have colleagues at work who are a bit irritating. We have our favorite TV shows and backyard gardens. There are trucks and trees, giraffes and toes. Our world is filled with fascinating stuff: some that we prefer, some that we'd rather avoid, and a lot that we don't even notice or know much about. Traditionally, all these experiences—this vast array of fascinating stuff—is said to be *no thing* or *empty,* in that, in reality, they are empty of *our* concepts and perspectives. When we commit to the present moment by coming back to our breath, we discover that we have not really been experiencing our world all along. Instead, we have been experiencing *our thoughts about the world.* When we leap into the present moment, we experience the world as *empty* of those thoughts: we experience our world directly rather than conceptually. We find that before we label our boss an "SOB," before we call a giraffe a "giraffe," and before we regard our phone as a friend or an enemy, this life and all our experiences are arising perfectly with no need for our waiting room preferences or labels. And it is this completely open and natural state, free of our preconceptions, that we commit to when we leap.

Experiencing the world on its empty terms rather than from our cozy bardo waiting room can be terrifying or brilliantly delightful—or both—because what we are engaging in very practical terms is utter uncertainty. Rather than offering us a fixed or tidy state of mind, the present moment reveals that our life is vivid, fluid, and constantly changing. What we had *thought* was solid and predictable is revealed as highly questionable. Our jobs; our identity; our financial security; indeed, our very lives are not guaranteed, and such uncertainty is front and center if we dare to commit to the present moment. Each time we come back to our breath, we gradually make friends with the fact that the essential nature of all that we experience—*the* basic and unavoidable fact of life—is that everything is constantly changing and therefore uncertain.

Typically, we live in dread of such reality, seeking to protect ourselves from life's instability, or what Buddhist teachers have called "groundlessness." We cannot tolerate the raw reality that death could happen at any moment or that our loved ones will depart or that we could lose our job tomorrow. But for mindful leaders, such rawness is what we leap into, and in so doing, we discover that in the uncertainty lies the very freedom we have been seeking all along. Remaining open in a world that is so inherently unpredictable demands courage and confidence in ourselves—the ability to trust that we are fully capable of being free—and it is precisely in such freedom that we rediscover our youthful delight and enthusiasm.

THE TALENT OF ENTHUSIASM

When the effort of leaping is extended from the cushion into our everyday life, we become willing to be abruptly here on the spot, living our lives fully with no guarantees. Traditionally, this willingness is called *virya*, or joyful vigor. Such energy is considered joyful because we are completely free to involve ourselves in our experience with no hesitation or rehearsing. We are joyfully engaged—like a kid working at a first job— rather than languishing in a sitting room. By engaging the immediacy of our lives, we naturally become intensely interested and open to life's ever-shifting creative patterns—vivid, fresh, and constantly changing.

For mindful leaders, then, work is not solely about meeting the obligations of paying the bills and getting the job done; it is much more about being free—connecting fully with our virya and expressing this inherent enthusiasm in our workplace. In the Tibetan tradition, expressing such delight is likened to how a snow lion inhabits the highlands of the Himalayas. The sky is bright and clear, and the snow among the foothills and forests is luminous and crisp. There is always a chill in the air of the present moment that keeps the lion perpetually alert and brisk. The lion is often seen leaping from boulder to boulder without hesitation, expressing a natural electricity and vigor in its movements. For mindful leaders, the freedom of leaping briskly and fully alert into the present moment like the Himalayan snow lion enables us to impact our workplace very directly with focus and skill.

First, since we experience a feeling of delight rather than burden, we naturally conduct ourselves artfully. We exhibit cunning—not in the sense of being deceptive or sneaky but in the sense of being intelligently engaged with whatever is happening. Rather than perpetually strategizing from behind a curtain and trying to get the upper hand in situations, mindful leaders, like the snow lion, freely engage the uncertainty of the situation as a fresh unknown, and we move according to what the circumstances demand. Such skillfulness is closely attuned to environmental cues, such as how an opponent negotiates or how confidently a subordinate expresses a point of view. For mindful leaders, such artful spontaneity is the source of all improvisation. Whatever arises—problematic, rewarding, shocking, or discouraging—we no longer pick and choose, but like a snow lion, we engage completely and adjust, adapt, and execute. We discover that by enthusiastically leaping into the present moment, we possess natural instincts that make us not only alert to whatever happens but also highly creative, able to artfully accommodate, challenge, and encourage.

Next, because we have the courage to open and leap into the present moment, our confidence grows stronger, and any doubts we harbor about our resourcefulness begin to wither. This is not to say that we begin to believe that we are infallible or simply glorious and wonderful—though, on occasion, for some of us this may be true. In this case, like the snow lion and the tiger, we are increasingly at ease with ourselves, no longer struggling to prove a point or win a battle. Such freedom from doubt eliminates the risk of all kinds of toxic missteps. Jealousy, arrogance, greed, and laziness all become pointless—at times, pathetic—approaches to engaging work and leading.

Finally, because we are no longer focused on protecting our job, prestige, and paycheck, we begin to tune in to how to be helpful to others. Our delight at being freely engaged with our work rather than enslaved by it introduces us to the pleasure of simply lending a hand. We all know the satisfaction we get from helping a colleague solve a problem or undertaking a successful initiative to improve the business. For mindful leaders, nourishing this impulse to help is at the very core of our youthful delight and enthusiasm. Since we are no longer afraid of our lives, we can freely open to others; because we no longer seek guarantees, we can be generous. By leaping into the present moment, we rediscover our long-lost youthful joy. And in the process, we find that such enthusiasm has been quietly resting within us all along.

10

PATIENCE

ABIDING IN THE PRESENT MOMENT

EVERY MORNING between 6:00 and 9:30 and every afternoon between 4:00 and 7:00, millions of people throughout the world engage in a uniquely human ritual called "rush hour." Visit just about any American urban area during these times and we find that rush hours across the country share many common features: the glow of brake lights from vehicles stopped on a highway; train stations bustling with commuters, coffee cups in hand; dozens of yellow taxis, trunks open, discharging passengers at airports. Traffic jams and packed subways, crowded lines and crammed parking lots—the ritual of the daily rush hour is a familiar aspect of our professional lives, fraught with tension, speed, and stress.

On the one hand, when we examine what we are doing during rush hour, it seems understandable: millions of us are just trying to get to work or get home simultaneously. As a New Yorker, I have marveled countless times at the amazing beauty and frenzy of the morning subway ritual—intense, packed, and chaotic. But the question that we may want to ask ourselves is "Why all the rush?"

Of course, the easy answer is that we want to be on time. We want to make our plane or attend a scheduled meeting. But the practical reality is that many, if not most, of us suffer dur-

ing rush hour: we are anxious, tense, and at times even resentful as we race to make an appointment or get to our desk at
the stipulated hour. A recent British study found that almost
half of working adults consider the rush hour commute the
single most stressful event of the workday, causing commuters
to suffer greater anxiety than fighter pilots or riot police.[1]
Essentially, rush hour is not so much an effort to be on time as
it is a ritual of frustration in which we feel under siege—and
we naturally want to hurry past such a negative experience and
on to something else—something more pleasant and productive. At rush hour, we are not just rushing *to* our job or home;
we are also *trying to rush past* the present moment, which reality will not permit.

To a great degree, rush hour reflects a much larger issue than
simply dashing to and from our jobs. We hurry through just
about everything: shopping, eating, schooling, exercising, even
making love. Many of us live a perpetual rush hour—scurrying through our lives, headed for somewhere else. Wait in line
at the grocery store for a moment "too long," for example, and
we can perceive our minds slowly coming to a boil, intolerant
of even the slightest brush with reality. How many of us have
found ourselves indignant and astonished when we get a busy
signal on the phone or realize in the midst of a purchase that
our credit card has expired?

One of my favorite commercials depicts a businessman
renting a car, but, bizarrely, we glimpse only a blur: the man
himself can't be seen. There is a blur of speed past the rental
counter, the resulting wind stirring the employee's hair. Again,
there is a blur of speed past the car attendant; past the rental
paperwork, which rustles in the breeze; and the blur shoots off
in a rented car. Throughout the commercial, all we see is a blur
of speed as employees look on a bit befuddled.

Finally, the blur arrives at its destination and slowly transforms into a smiling customer on vacation with a golf bag over
his shoulder as the voice-over proclaims, "National Car Rental:
Faster than the speed of life."

Now, National Car Rental actually does a pretty good job of
offering safe, affordable cars for rent at accessible locations. But
its marketing pitch touted more than just safety, affordability,
and efficiency. Its commercial portrayed life as a perpetual rush
hour, and if we listen closely to what National was actually saying in its ad, we would hear a clear message: "National Car
Rental: Speeding conveniently past reality en route to somewhere else—it's a way of life!"

In the final analysis, the National Car Rental commercial
shows how all of us too often live our lives as a blur—rushing
past our families; jobs; friends; and, yes, rental car employees—trying to get somewhere else fast rather than being where
we are, trying to become someone else rather than being who
we are, trying to hurry past the reality of nowness rather than
waking up to it. And for mindful leaders, living in such a perpetual rush hour only condemns us to a life of disappointment
and exhaustion in which we struggle to find meaning in a fee-
ble culture of impatience—frustrated with our lives and resentful of others, taking our disappointment out on a world that
appears to be in our way.

ABIDING IN THE PRESENT MOMENT

Mindfulness meditation involves acknowledging our state of
mind, letting go of thoughts and emotions of all kinds, and
bringing our attention to the present moment. Traditionally, the

method for sustaining our attention in the present moment is attending mindfully to our breath, as explained by the Buddha in his original instruction to his monks and nuns, recorded in the Anapanasati sutra:

> There is the case where a monk, having gone to the wilderness, to the shade of a tree, or to an empty building, sits down folding his legs crosswise, holding his body erect, and setting mindfulness to the fore. Always mindful, he breathes in; mindful he breathes out. Breathing in long, he discerns that he is breathing in long; or breathing out long, he discerns that he is breathing out long. Or breathing in short, he discerns that he is breathing in short; or breathing out short, he discerns that he is breathing out short. He trains himself to breathe in sensitive to the entire body, and to breathe out sensitive to the entire body. He trains himself to breathe in calming the bodily processes, and to breathe out calming the bodily processes.[2]

Attending to our breath, always mindful as it goes in and always mindful as it goes out, as the Buddha suggests here, is pretty straightforward. There is no magic power or yogic gymnastic. There is no drama or special apparel we must wear. In fact, if we practice mindfulness regularly and for extended periods, we will inevitably notice that attending to our breath—indeed, the entire process of meditating—is tremendously boring.

On the surface of things, it seems easy to see why sitting still for hours on end attending to the breath as it goes in and out would be boring. Nothing is happening. We aren't accomplishing anything; we're not going anywhere or having any fun. We may start out thinking that by meditating, we could overcome stress and develop enlightened states of mind, but instead, when we practice mindfulness meditation, we find that absolutely nothing is going on.

At first, such a discovery can be quite disturbing, and we can find ourselves "freaking out" on the cushion. I recall a sinister little trick meditation teachers would pull when conducting *dathun,* a monthlong meditation retreat in which participants sit for eight to ten hours a day. Each day, sitting would end during a final session beginning at 7:00 in the evening. But the sinister little trick was that each evening session could last anywhere from forty-five minutes to two hours. So, as soon as the clock reached 7:45, the pressure would build. "When are they going to ring the gong to end the session?" I would think. "They are up to something—I know it—they are going to have us sit until midnight. But wait a minute—maybe the session is about to end!" Back and forth—hope and fear. I, for one, would always freak out a bit toward the end of a long day of sitting.

Eventually, however, if we persevere, we stop freaking out and begin to make friends with boredom. We discover that we are learning how to abide in the present moment. Rather than living in a perpetual rush hour, blurring past our lives, we learn by sitting on the cushion how to slow down and wake up to who and where we are, very directly, with no excuses or distractions. My teacher, Chögyam Trungpa, put great emphasis on cultivating a healthy, firm relationship with boredom. He taught that by having the courage to be bored on the cushion, we can learn to appreciate our minds and to live our lives properly and thoroughly. "It is a good feeling to be bored," he said, "constantly sitting and sitting. First gong, second gong, third gong, more gongs to come. Sit, sit, sit, sit . . . until the boredom becomes extraordinarily powerful. We have to work hard at it."[3]

Working hard at being bored may sound absurd, maybe even offensive, but this is exactly what we do when we sit on the cushion and abide in the present moment. We take our posture, gather our minds, and sit. As thoughts and emotions arise, we acknowledge them by labeling them "thinking." Then we let go, open, and "whoooshhh," as my teacher would say, into the present moment. Our senses alert, our body relaxed, and our attention placed lightly on our breath, we just sit. Our mind, body, and the phenomenal world synchronize as a singular unfolding moment, and we sit—gently aware of our breath. The soft scent of incense, the shadows on the floor, a cat lazily strolling across the room—everything arises perfectly in its boring simplicity, and we just sit.

By abiding in the present moment with such unshakable boredom, we discover at some point that we are not meditating at all and in fact we were never meditating in the first place. We discover that what we were doing all along was *just sitting*—quite literally. The technique of labeling and following the breath falls away, and we understand clearly and directly what it means to simply sit. When our boredom transforms into just sitting, we discover what Zen Buddhism calls *nyu nan shin*, or smooth natural mind: natural because our mind rests in its original state and smooth because it is essentially composed. When we permit ourselves to merely sit, we are at our ease abiding in the present moment, and for mindful leaders, such natural ease is the source of all skill and power.

THE TALENT OF PATIENCE

When we bring the boredom of *abiding in the present moment* into our everyday life, we learn how to manage expectations— our own and others'. Unlike being in a perpetual rush hour, in which we are constantly attempting to get somewhere else, mindful leaders attend to the present moment and are willing to deal realistically with whatever occurs. We understand that life's circumstances are uncertain, and because of that, we do not sell false hopes or dread inevitable problems. Rather, the unshakable presence that comes from being bored on the cushion grounds us in the realities of life, in which we have no choice but to deal with exactly what is happening. And in the same way as we are comfortable *just sitting,* we are at our ease engaging whatever arises.

This is not to say that when tragedy strikes, we are stone-faced or act like clinical robots. Nor does such realism require us to remain stoic when we win the million-dollar lottery. Instead, as mindful leaders, we are willing to engage each experience precisely on its own terms with all the sadness and joy, all the humor and passion, the circumstances demand. Rather than living in anticipation of what might happen next—hoping for the best and fearing the worst—we discard such crude expectations and resourcefully engage our circumstances on the terms that arise in the present moment. Traditionally, such willingness to work with whatever may happen is called *kshanti,* or patience, and for mindful leaders, such patience is how we engage our emotions intelligently at work.

Typically, we experience our emotions as colorful recollections and internal dramas. We reflect on a pleasant moment with our loved ones, and we savor the emotion of affection and contentment. Or we ponder a distasteful experience with a colleague in which we felt insulted and mistreated, and we dramatize the emotions of anger and shame. Kshanti, however, introduces us to emotions not as recollections or internal dramas but as how we experience the present moment. Because we are synchronized, we are not trapped rehearsing our emotions as colorful discursive dialogue. Instead, we *live* our emotions and begin to understand their natural intelligence. Humor arises because the situation is funny; concern arises because the situation warrants careful consideration; kindness is offered because the situation invites gentleness. Such emotional naturalness is due to the awareness we develop by abiding patiently in the present moment. Kshanti shows us that if we are willing to be open and authentic with our world, we can be free to experience emotions as they arise rather than rehearsing them as overexaggerated dramas.

Because we are emotionally freed from dramatizing or repressing our emotions, we are not easily impressed by emotional tantrums, impoverishment, or arrogance when they are displayed at work. As mindful leaders, we understand in very immediate terms the weakness of such a rush-hour mentality, and we are willing to engage it skillfully and systematically rather than trying to mud-wrestle it into submission. Traditionally, one of the great benefits of kshanti is said to be the ability "to be favorably inclined toward inconsiderate and harmful people." Because we have had the courage and patience to unravel our own arrogance and anxiety, we are favorably inclined to do so with others.

Finally, the patience we cultivate on the cushion unfolds in our lives as a willingness to drop our anger toward life's inconveniences, hardships, and injustices. As mindful leaders, we know that life will deal us many difficult hands. We know that our work and career—our home life and spiritual path—will encounter innumerable setbacks and disappointments. While such hardships may challenge us greatly, patience teaches us that anger is not necessary; in fact, it only confuses matters further. As mindful leaders, our boredom teaches us to work with whatever arises without resentment. And because we are patient and free from anger, we are willing to run a country or empty a bedpan, launch a new product or lay off an entire department. Since we are not rushing past our lives, we deal with each circumstance precisely and patiently, and no detail is beneath us.

11

AWARENESS

GLIMPSING OPEN SPACE

HIRING the right people to get the job done is central in any organization, and identifying the needed mix of skills and attitudes is as much art as it is science. For example, hiring capable information technology (IT) talent is always a challenge. New, highly specialized technologies are emerging in every field, from medicine to military defense to finance, requiring increasingly customized expertise. So it is little wonder in our modern economy that IT professionals are highly sought after for their *technical* skills. But ask any CIO what prevents most IT professionals from succeeding, and you will not hear stories of technical failure. Rather, you will hear accounts of project managers unable to build consensus within a team, systems development directors unable to establish rapport with clients, and technology officers unable to communicate in simple, understandable terms. In the case of IT professionals, as with so many of us in the workplace, technical skills are not enough to get the job done. In order to succeed, we also need a broader set of skills and perspectives— we also need *awareness*.

Helping employees develop such workplace awareness beyond technical know-how is vital, for without it, employees lose their motivation, organizational cultures calcify, and mediocrity becomes acceptable. For example, many of us are familiar with starting a new job enthusiastically—ready to get the work done—only to become demoralized and disoriented within the first several months, and it is not the technical aspects of our jobs that are so discouraging. Poor communications with the boss, political missteps, inadequate orientation, infrequent supervision, and conflicts with colleagues—the list of culprits is quite long and undoubtedly familiar. And such initial discouragement with a new job continues for years afterward. Of course, much of the responsibility here rests with management. However, regardless of whether our efforts are supported by skillful management and healthy organizations, all of us must cultivate, for our own sake, the awareness to prosper and contribute at work beyond our technical abilities.

Over the past several decades, scholars and business professionals have tried to identify what distinguishes aware, capable performers from those who merely deliver technically, and the difference seems to come down to this: technicians focus on getting it right; those with workplace awareness are attuned to what happens around them *as* they get it right. Research has found that we are technically effective *only* to the degree to which we can influence the setting in which we work. Organizations employ diverse types of people, with various agendas, functioning in multilayered social milieus, which necessitates our being distinctly *aware* of how we impact such a complex environment. Such insight involves much more than just "getting it right."

Consequently, success requires not only technical skills but also a wide range of sophisticated "awareness competencies," such as being comfortable with ambiguity, skillfully questioning the status quo, understanding the political impact of one's actions and words, communicating complex ideas to diverse groups, and much more. Those who demonstrate these awareness competencies are more likely to listen, adapt, speak straightforwardly, and be authentic, and such awareness has been shown to distinguish superior performers and leaders from those who struggle simply to get it right.

Understanding that we must be intelligently aware at work is one thing, but demonstrating such awareness is a much greater challenge. Like our IT professionals, many of us find ourselves under great pressure to deliver technically at work, and when it comes to such skills as listening better, resolving conflicts, or building rapport, there just doesn't seem to be the time or support.

Mindful leaders cannot dispense with developing this workplace awareness, however, because it rests firmly on our willingness to make friends with ourselves. Usually, we think of awareness in conceptual terms, such as being smart or qualified; but in this case, the awareness of mindful leaders is experiential—an emotional and physical comfort with our state of mind that broadens into a penetrating familiarity with the complex world around us. Such awareness, then, begins with getting to know ourselves—a self-awareness that is honest, open, and accurate. As Daniel Goleman, author of *Emotional Intelligence,* writes:

> Self-awareness is the first component of emotional intelligence. . . . Self-awareness means having a deep understanding of one's emotions, strengths, weaknesses, needs and drives. People with strong self-awareness are neither overly critical nor unrealistically

hopeful. Rather, they are honest—with themselves and others. People who have a high degree of self-awareness recognize how their feelings affect them, other people and their job performance. . . . It shows itself as candor and an ability to assess oneself realistically. People with high self-awareness are able to speak accurately and openly . . . about their emotions and the impact they have on their work.[1]

Mindful leaders cultivate such intelligent self-awareness on the cushion. Engaging our minds in mindfulness meditation reveals that we can be in tune with who we are—honest, open, and confident. Such mindfulness or self-awareness naturally opens further into a wider wakefulness—a wisdom that is personal and intimate yet vastly profound and skillful.

GLIMPSING OPEN SPACE

As we deepen our mindfulness practice on the cushion, we become increasingly relaxed with the boredom of it all. No longer do we struggle with our emotions; instead, we become comfortable with the simplicity of *just sitting*—abiding in the present moment. Our commitment to sitting still and simply *being* gradually becomes powerful, firm, and reliable, and we relax into our natural state of being. Such natural firmness does not struggle with emotions as if they were unruly children or relate with the body as if it were a separate event. Rather, we relax into what is traditionally called nondual awareness wisdom, or *prajna*.

Prajna is not wisdom in the conventional sense of being

unusually experienced, exhibiting encyclopedic knowledge, being able to offer good advice, or being infallible. Rather, nondual awareness wisdom is the natural outcome of discovering through mindfulness that there is no inherent distinction between our mind, our body, and the phenomenal world. Prajna arises as a kind of physical wisdom of being in the present moment in which our mindfulness transforms into awareness: we shift from being *mindful of* what is occurring to being *aware in* what is occurring.

Such a shift into nondual awareness wisdom is quite natural, offering what is traditionally called a panoramic view. Imagine for a moment that you have recently moved to an unfamiliar large city such as New York. At first, the whole metropolis seems so vast and unknowable. Every corner is crowded with thousands of faces, and nothing seems familiar. Uptown, downtown; SoHo, Upper West Side, Central Park—the entire display is rich and colorful yet distinctly disorienting. But luckily, you have your apartment and your new job—you have something to work with and focus on.

When you go to work for the first couple of weeks, you take the same path to the same train at the same time, and you become familiar with your simple routine. As with your mindfulness practice, you are precise and repetitive and thorough. You may still feel disoriented by the city's vibrant chaos, but your mindfulness keeps you focused.

One day, a colleague at work invites you over to her apartment for dinner, and she lives in a part of the city that you have not yet visited. So you mindfully take out the subway map and chart a course for getting to her home. This time when you go to the subway, you take a different path, catch a different train, and arrive at a different location. Even though you still feel disoriented in this new city, the precision of your mindfulness permits you to find your way. As you exit the subway station and emerge onto the New York streets, you naturally try to get your bearings. Everything is still new and unfamiliar, but as you look around, you notice the Empire State Building, which you have seen many times before on your way to work. Normally, however, you viewed the skyscraper from the north looking south, but now you are seeing it for the first time from the south looking north, and you suddenly say to yourself, "Hey, I know where I am!" You experience a sudden shift from being *mindful of* your circumstances to being *aware in* your circumstances. Your mind and body "synchronize" with the spacious city around you, and your "knowing" suddenly and naturally becomes larger—panoramic.

This shift, in which we suddenly become oriented in seemingly unknown circumstances, is very similar to how the wisdom of prajna dawns in our mindfulness practice. After hours, weeks, months, and years of attending precisely to our mindfulness technique, we find that we no longer need to keep track because we know where we are. This knowing, or prajna wisdom, is quite physical, in which the immediacy of what we are experiencing, the environment or space around the experience, and ourselves as the experiencer all simultaneously harmonize as a singular, undifferentiated moment. We glimpse that who we are, where we are, is not a matter of what we think but is a vivid awareness that unfolds in all directions—a wisdom that had been accompanying us all along as background that suddenly reveals itself as a radiant foreground.

Traditionally, such radiant wisdom is likened to the panoramic view of a *garuda,* a kind of magical eagle. The garuda soars high in the sky with a vast view in all directions. But the garuda does not comment on its view; it does not take notes or remark to itself, "Hey, isn't this a wonderfully clear day—I can see my nest from here!" Rather, the garuda experiences no distinction between itself, the vast sky, and its panoramic view. The garuda is at its ease careening through infinite space, synchronized with the sky, the earth below, and its vision. Such is the wisdom of prajna, and for the mindful leader, bringing such wisdom to the workplace is a practical matter that has the highest priority.

THE TALENT OF AWARENESS

Bringing the awareness we discover on the cushion into our everyday life requires that we slow down and notice what is happening around us—not just once, but dozens of times a day. By slowing down in this way, we widen our mindfulness practice into panoramic awareness, appreciating the space around what we are doing. This does not mean that at work, we suddenly stop in the hallway and go into some kind of trance or sit meditation in the bathroom. We don't tell our colleagues that we are taking a break to imagine ourselves as a magical eagle flying high over our office building. Rather, we bring the talent of awareness into our everyday life by simply glimpsing that we are synchronized with our world right here, right now, on the spot. Many subtle instructions have been offered down through the centuries for invoking this nondual awareness wisdom, but essentially, they involve stopping the mind, noticing the situation, synchronizing, and then letting go—exactly what we do on the cushion.

Engendering this awareness at work is highly practical,

because it is how mindful leaders develop the much-needed awareness competencies required to successfully get the work done. When we permit prajna to inform us at work, we don't just do our jobs technically; we also appreciate the space around our jobs, just like suddenly getting our bearings in a seemingly vast city.

Typically, we are not comfortable with space: we prefer focusing on activity and on getting things "technically" done. One of my favorite tricks to pull on people who attend my lectures and seminars is to introduce someone who never arrives. I mention that on the plane coming to the seminar, I unexpectedly met an expert, Dr. So-and-So, who kindly agreed to come and address us briefly on the topic of space. Then, asking everyone to welcome Dr. So-and-So, I gesture toward the stage door in anticipation of the doctor's arrival—and nothing happens. No one arrives except silence, which slowly, like an invisible spreading breeze, permeates the entire room: five seconds, ten seconds, twenty seconds—just pure silent space. At the end of this little exercise, I ask the audience what just happened, and the consensus always is that people were becoming anxious, uncomfortable, and even worried about Dr. So-and-So's not arriving. "Why do we become anxious?" I ask. "What's wrong with a little space once in a while? Just because Dr. So-and-So can't be here doesn't mean that we can't."

Mindful leaders are not anxious when experiencing a larger, more spacious view, and such comfort is an outgrowth of our mindfulness practice. Rather than narrowly focusing on how tasks arrive on our workplace stage, we expand our perspective and also appreciate the stage itself—the larger organizational and human context in which we find ourselves. As mindful leaders, we view work from the garuda's perspective, understanding the broader impact *as* we engage work's demands: we recognize options; appreciate nuances; explore unseen possibilities; and, yes, gently value silence. Such a view gives us a maneuverability and political awareness that permit us to relax with *how* we conduct ourselves rather than rushing through our tasks in hopes of achieving our goals. Traditionally, this awareness of the garuda is said to unfold in everyday life in two ways: the wisdom of knowing and the wisdom of seeing.

The wisdom of knowing arises when we drop our addiction to rehearsing our emotions as mental dramas and instead permit our feelings to rest in their natural state, which is a physical instinctual knowing. We all use phrases such as "I've got a gut feeling" or "my intuition tells me" to describe this wisdom of physically knowing. If we examine our emotions closely, we will notice that they are, in fact, bodily sensations that are occurring in the present moment and guiding us in a particular direction. Typically, we remain unaware of our emotions as physical sensations because we spend most of our time rehearsing and distorting them into internal spectacles. Our mindfulness practice, however, gradually releases this artificial grasp we exert on our emotions, and we learn to viscerally trust our feelings and discover that we can "know" the situation directly.

This wisdom of knowing is our ability to "get" what is going on rather than "figure it out," know where we are rather than just track the details, intuit immediately the substance of a situation rather than rely on rationally cataloging the pros and cons. Such a perspective offers a broader and more mature range of possibilities when dealing with work's circumstances —indeed, when dealing with life in general. This wisdom that we develop on the cushion is how we move past "getting the job done" to "getting the job done *intelligently*." Instead of being a distraction from our job, our emotions unfold as a wisdom of knowing when to listen and when to speak, when to help and when to refrain, when to direct and when to follow.

The wisdom of seeing is our ability to glimpse reality. Because we are first open to our experience rather than obsessed with imposing our opinions, we bring a fresh and unbiased mind to whatever occurs. This is not to say that we don't still have ideas about what to cook for dinner or which might be the most successful product to launch. Instead, seeing wisely is permitting our world to totally absorb us—capture our full attention—an attention that is so committed that we no longer catalog our experience or keep it at arm's length. We are fully engaged with whatever is happening, and because we are so present, we can glimpse the nature of things directly.

For mindful leaders, this wisdom of seeing does not distinguish between the mundane and the sublime. Whether we are falling in love or taking out the garbage, this wisdom reveals directly that we are fully synchronized with what we are doing and can therefore penetrate to the very core of what is occurring. We could, for example, be trying to resolve a conflict between two colleagues who are heatedly debating each other's shortcomings, and because we are willing to be totally available, we glimpse exactly what's going on. We see quite literally the embarrassment and wounded heart of one colleague as she arrogantly defends herself and dismisses the other. And we see the panic of her colleague as he tries to remain cool under fire, putting the best face on an insult he never intended to deliver. Our willingness to be totally present to our lives reveals that we have a remarkable power to see directly into the hearts and

minds of others, and such seeing offers mindful leaders tremendous possibilities for helping and contributing.

Finally, the wisdom of seeing also reveals time and again that
our experience in the present moment is unspeakably profound and that our humanity springs from a primordial clarity so vast yet so personal that we have no option but to remain
humble. Gaining confidence in such profound insight is a
source of great joy for mindful leaders, offering the possibility
of being cheerful under all circumstances.

12

SKILLFULNESS
EXTENDING OUT OFF THE CUSHION

"Y JOB is to get from point A to point B as directly and as quickly as possible" was how a scientist client once described her job to me. And while being so straightforwardly effective at work is important, it is by no means sufficient. We may get to point B, but *how* we get there makes all the difference in the world. In a certain sense, making the right decisions, being competent, staying on course, and getting the job done is the easy part. The hard part is being skillful in the process.

Being skillful at work can mean many things. A doctor who performs complex feats of brain surgery, a cabinetmaker who seamlessly joins fine wood, and an accountant who makes even the most convoluted tax returns look easy can all be said to be "skillful." In this case, we are not speaking of the skill of a craftsman or the ability of an artist. The skillfulness of mindful leaders is how we inspire the best in others—it's how we arrive at point B with our collective sanity and dignity intact.

Throughout my career, I have marveled repeatedly at how unskillful I and others have been at work. We put so much effort into getting from point A to point B, but somehow, upon our arrival, we find ourselves surrounded by alienated clients, stressed-out employees, and resentful colleagues. Such a scenario is the result of unskillful leadership, in which gaining emotional victory and *displaying* success outweigh actually succeeding.

I once attended a meeting during my publishing career that illustrates this point in very crude terms. The fiscal year was coming to a close, and for the most part, all the publishing company's divisions were delivering smartly on their business plans. Profits were higher, sales were up, new technology was unfolding, and the company was leading in most markets. There was much to be proud of.

As was standard business procedure, each division's management team journeyed to headquarters to present its fourth-quarter results and discuss next year's projections. The ritual was well known—and somewhat dreaded—throughout the company. The division's management would troop in, sit on one side of the boardroom table, and face off against a team of corporate officers, which included the company's most senior executives. The division management would make a presentation, and the corporate officers would ask questions—and inevitably make demands. I did not attend such meetings often, and when I did, I found them fascinating and intelligent. People knew their customers and competitors; they were thoughtful in their planning and clever in their creative impulse. Yet there was always someone "waiting in the weeds" ready to ambush even the most successful work.

In this particular case, a publishing team arrived and made its presentation. Exciting new products were splashed across the screen, and colorful, engaging marketing plans were reviewed. To top it off, fourth-quarter profits and sales were above projection. People were pumped, excited, and pretty proud of themselves.

Of course, there was discussion about next year's projections. The division was performing so well, maybe it could do more: deliver more sales, higher profits. Despite this pressure to raise their numbers, all those in the room remained collegial and somewhat playful, given the solid results already delivered—until a senior financial executive who had remained relatively quiet throughout the presentation concluded the meeting with a droll, sarcastic remark directed at the division management: "Well, I guess we can end the meeting now, since you're obviously sandbagging us. Like I said all along, you guys are just coasting, and we should have asked for more money—and maybe we still will." With that, he stood and left the room.

I'll never forget the sense of sudden defeat that filled the air. Lightness had grown heavy; open had gone closed; self-respect and inspiration had turned sour. And it all happened in a matter of seconds. Here was an executive team that had delivered millions of dollars in profit, exceeded most of its business goals, beat the competition, and produced excellent products, and one colleague in need of *displaying an emotional victory* tidily summed up such results as an insult—"sandbagging": no appreciation, no gratitude, no inspiration. While it was a distinctly distasteful experience, I wouldn't have traded it for the world. For in a flash, I had learned quite viscerally that arriving successfully at point B can easily be transformed into a toxic event simply by being unskillful.

Although this rude story is a bit extreme, it is unfortunately not unusual in today's workplace. Being emotionally careless and unskillful at work—bullying, gossip, personal harassment, rigid stubbornness—appears to be at epidemic proportions, and many of us find ourselves, at times, the unwitting authors of such carelessness.

Traditionally, handling situations skillfully rather than being careless and emotionally sloppy is considered a central task of the mindful leader, and such skillfulness is referred to as *upaya*—literally, appropriate or skillful means. Essentially, upaya is our natural ability to appreciate what each situation needs, adapt our perspective in order to bring about the best results, and then act accordingly. But being skillful has less to do with the situation we are trying to manage than with the mind-set we bring to the challenge. Upaya first and foremost demands that we drop our schemes for emotional victory at work. We may say that we just want to achieve results, to get the job done, to do what is right. But too often, such motives are not the whole story. We not only want to get from point A to point B, but we also want the emotional rewards that come with arriving *our* way, on *our* schedule, on *our* terms. When we take this perspective—unconsciously or not—workplace circumstances can appear more complicated than they are. Slights are amplified into grave business challenges; mistakes are exaggerated into intentional threats; routine accomplishments are stage-managed as heroics. Normal, run-of-the-mill problems are viewed as emergencies, and simple achievements are sugarcoated and overdramatized. Upaya reveals such struggle for emotional victory as pointlessly distracting us from the real issues at hand.

Workplace challenges are almost always simpler or more complex than we are willing to admit, and upaya opens us to these possibilities. When we are skillful, we understand that what we must accomplish has little to do with achieving *emotional gratification* and far more to do with helping others achieve what is necessary. Our financial executive needed to prove a point emotionally, demonstrate dominance, and keep others on tenterhooks—and such an agenda served no one. By dropping any need for emotional victory, we become open to truly understanding what the situation calls for and expressing to others a natural sense of warmth and appreciation, the central impulse of being skillful.

EXTENDING OUT OFF THE CUSHION

As with everything in life, even a meditation session on the cushion comes to an end. We may sit for fifteen minutes or an hour or maybe longer, but how we end the session requires attention and skill.

Typically, we end a session of meditation with some kind of signal: maybe a colleague strikes a gong or our alarm beeps. Suddenly, our effort at attending precisely to the breath and abiding gently in the present moment is seemingly interrupted, and we begin thinking about what to do next. We may have a busy day ahead of us or a difficult challenge to address. Or maybe we are leaving on a vacation to Rajasthan and feeling quite excited. Such thoughts and feelings may come as a flood or a whisper, but they nonetheless arise quite naturally. If we permit these thoughts to rush in too quickly, we will inevitably tighten and close off. At exactly this point, we can drop the effort of considering what's next and once again bring our attention back very gently to the simple vividness of the present moment. We just rest, *with no technique,* and permit our mindfulness to relax naturally and take in the full measure of whatever is occurring.

Slowly, we begin to shift our bodies, maybe stretch our backs and legs out a bit. If we are sitting with others, we may notice fellow meditators rising from their cushions or just catch a glimpse of snow falling outside the window. If we are attentive as we make this shift, we will experience a distinct sense of expanding relief. We are finished with our sitting session, and an easy unfolding occurs—as if we were taking a long, deep inhalation and releasing it with a sigh of "aah." Such relief is a further expanding of the openness we have been cultivating throughout our meditation and is tinged with a sense of tenderness and joy. Like a child let out of school, we expand out with delight. We are released from the claustrophobia of "technique," and there are things to do—much is possible. Yet, like a child, we are also uncontrived and nakedly curious, which has a distinct sense of tenderness. If we notice carefully, we are quite exposed at this point as we transition to our everyday life off the cushion, and remaining at our ease and not rushing past the simple rawness takes a gentle touch.

Traditionally, such raw, tender openness is called *bodhi citta,* which means awake or genuine heart. When we first start practicing mindfulness meditation, we quickly notice this tender heart of bodhi citta, and it is not unusual to think that something is wrong. We feel as if our heart were broken, and our life seems so sore and raw. Everywhere we look, everything we reach out to seems to penetrate us—almost as if we have a wound that keeps reopening. Typically, we struggle against such rawness: we want to feel happy and strong, not tender and sore. We might actually live our lives trying to cover up this tenderness, feeling embarrassed by our lives and looking for emotional victories that seem to hold the promise of security. But mindfulness reveals that life offers and demands intimacy, and with that comes the simple tenderness of being human.

Over time, we discover through mindfulness that this tenderness is not a problem but has been with us every step of the way throughout our lives. For whatever reasons, all of us have been touched by life, and in a very real sense, our hearts have been broken. Mindful leaders do not regard this tenderness as a problem or tragedy but as something to be cultivated, and gradually, as we open, we notice that there is remarkable warmth unfolding in our lives—a natural sympathy or appreciation toward whatever is occurring. Such warmth creates tremendous space for us and others because there is no impulse to protect ourselves or hold back in embarrassment. We find that we harbor no resentment toward life's impositions and consequently experience no need for emotional victory, which is an extremely powerful point of view.

But this tenderness does not stand on its own, for it functions as a foundation for our intelligence, or prajna, to curiously inspect and engage situations. The warmth we develop in mindfulness does not turn us into a charitable organization or create a permanent inclination to feel sorry for others. Rather, such natural warmth extends out toward others as appreciation, creating an atmosphere in which there is no need for aggression or panic or fear. Instead of complicating workplace circumstances with our need for emotional victory, our warmth openly advertises for all to see that emotional victory is pointless. Such openness sets the stage for us to be genuinely curious and inviting—which, not surprisingly, inspires others to be so as well.

Being aware of this warmth as we transition from our cushion to our everyday activities is extremely important, for such warmth is the basis for upaya—how we can be skillful in our lives. The warmth we develop on the cushion is how we reduce our need for emotional victories and in turn skillfully inspire others to do the same.

THE TALENT OF SKILLFULNESS

When we combine our awareness and natural warmth at work, we find that we can inspire others—even in the most difficult situations. Our warmth tends to melt away the rigid resistance of fear and aggression that often confuses our daily circumstances. People may come to a meeting with a defensive attitude, or they may want to take advantage of us in a negotiation; they may be suspicious of our motives or overly complimentary, but as mindful leaders, we are not deeply perturbed by such things—there is no need for theatrics, anger, or embarrassment. Instead, we naturally extend an atmosphere of genuine appreciation—creating a tone that is welcoming and powerfully open. This is not to say that we are inappropriately tolerant, permitting others to mistreat, falsely accuse, or deride us. Rather, since we are not seeking emotional victory, we can open to such difficulties and be *spontaneously* inquisitive. There are no staged remarks delivered for effect or insights shared in order to impress. There is no need for bullying or one-upmanship. The intelligent curiosity of mindful leaders does not wait in the weeds ready to ambush with all kinds of arrogant charades. The intelligence of upaya is sharply transparent and has only one motive—to inspire the best in the circumstances. Such sharpness may not always be comfortable, for it can cut quickly to the heart of an issue, eliminate unnecessary noise, or probe into areas that others would prefer remain unexamined. On the other hand, such sharpness can inspire others to speak their mind, take a risk that needs to be taken, or consider options that would normally appear threatening. As mindful leaders, the sharp intelligence of prajna is how we perform our jobs, and the warmth of bodhi citta's tenderness is how we humanize our leadership. Such is the spontaneous nature of upaya—being skillful.

Traditionally, mindful leaders sharpen skillful intelligence and deepen the tender warmth by contemplating the *four immeasurables:* respect, genuine caring, delight, and impartiality. These four "contemplative reminders" act as a kind of air conditioner that continually refreshes and cleanses our state of mind, helping us remain open and appreciative throughout the day.

Respect

Though we may want to envision ourselves as entrepreneurs or self-made persons, the reality is that many people contribute to our well-being. Consider any object on which we rely—car, fresh water from the spigot, cotton undergarments. Thousands of hardworking people from around the world make these possible for us and are worthy of our respect. As mindful leaders, we extend such appreciation to our workplace as well. Like us, our colleagues are trying to be successful; they are trying to do their best; they, too, want to be inspired and live a decent, dignified life. Such aspiration is worthy of our respect.

Genuine Caring

Everyone suffers at times. We lose our loved ones, or we become burdened with physical illnesses or mental trauma. At times, we become lost and uninspired by life. Appreciating such distress is how mindful leaders stay open and wise. Of course, such genuine caring does not mean that we are going to solve everyone's problems or spend all day contemplating how painful life is. Rather, because we are mindful leaders, we naturally open to others and inevitably witness their suffering. And instead of ignoring or dismissing it, we fully taste it—we genuinely care.

Delight

Each day, millions of people succeed: they fall in love, invent a new lifesaving drug, pass an exam, or just stroll through a favorite park. As mindful leaders, we do not take people for granted: the hardworking accountant, the creative marketing analyst, the thorough sales rep. We actually take the time to appreciate others' positive qualities and contributions and delight in their success.

Impartiality

Normally, we prefer being respectful of those we like, we genuinely care for those with whom we are familiar, and we delight in the successes of those we support. Mindful leaders, however, find that such preferences are too narrow and exclude many who are in need of our help and inspiration. We strive, then, to extend our respect, genuine caring, and delight impartially—with openness toward all. We may drop our resistance to a particularly irritating colleague at work who is constantly complaining and wish her well on her new promotion, or we may contemplate the millions of people we have never met who suffer terribly throughout the day. Such impartiality treats all with equal skill and respect regardless of their station or distance.

In the end, the skillfulness of mindful leaders is how we drop our addiction to emotional victories of all kinds. We may be confronting a disastrous business deal or a successful sale, a conflict with our boss or a new and promising partnership—no matter the circumstances, as mindful leaders, we shed any emotional carelessness and instead openly appreciate our circumstances with no agenda other than our natural warmth and intelligent curiosity.

13

HUMILITY

DISSOLVING THE FIXED SENSE OF SELF AND OTHERS

As I passed by the room of my high school son, Hayden, one afternoon, I noticed him excitedly peering over the shoulder of his friend Daniel into the screen of his computer as Daniel typed away frantically at the keyboard. I watched for a moment as they eagerly exchanged comments:

"What did she say?" asked Hayden excitedly.

"Nothing yet—I'm still waiting," responded Daniel.

"Do you think she got the message?" Hayden probed.

"I don't know, but her friend Nicole seems cool," he replied.

I proceeded on my way accomplishing a few chores and came back to discover Hayden and his friend still mesmerized.

"Hey, guys, what are you doing?" I asked.

Turning their heads and without missing a beat, they responded in unison, "We're talking to girls!"

"Talking to girls?" I responded. "On a computer? How's that work?"

And they proceeded to give me a quick, impassioned tutorial on chat rooms. Apparently, my son and his friend had discovered a local digital meeting place where high school kids congregated to swap stories, spread gossip, and build friendships. But it was not as simple as it appeared.

"The problem is that the girls won't talk to the boys," explained my son, puzzling over an age-old dilemma.

"So, you know what we decided to do, Mr. Carroll," chimed in Daniel. "We are pretending to be girls," he whispered, "and now the girls will talk to us."

A small alarm was beginning to ring somewhere in the back of my mind when my son quietly mumbled, "But now we have a bigger problem."

"And what's that?" I asked.

"Well, Mr. Carroll," Daniel responded with a puzzled look on his face, "now that we're pretending to be girls and the girls are talking to us, we can't tell who we're talking to—*girls,* or *boys* pretending to be girls. . . ."

"We're kinda getting a little confused!" puzzled my son as both he and Daniel stared at me in naive distress.

Needless to say, I could not help but laugh out loud, and to this day, remembering the story always brings a fresh smile to my face. But this little tale about confusion in a teenage chat room reflects a greater challenge that we all face at work and throughout our lives in general—the challenge of genuine communication.

To some degree, we all find ourselves living a part of our lives in a chat room in which, in order to reach out to colleagues and strangers, even lovers and friends, we disguise ourselves—pretending to be someone we are not. Sometimes, like my son and his friend Daniel, we just want to be appreciated or just want to talk, and we assume a guise that allows us to say hello. Or sometimes we may want to be seen as powerful and importantly busy and we project an air of entitlement and studied self-assurance. Or maybe we don't feel so confident at all, so we don a costume of indifference or fawning compliance.

The wardrobes we affect—particularly at work—are fairly predictable: the ambitious expert, the aloof executive, the rigid perfectionist, the frenzied go-getter. We know them well because we all, to some degree, have played the part. For mindful leaders, however, such costumes, while understandable, can be the source of great confusion at work, because, in the end, by communicating through costumes, we find ourselves in a chat room, unable to distinguish authentic communication from mere charade.

When we communicate through our credentials, ideology, or celebrity, we run the risk of sending mixed messages. On the one hand, we want human contact—we want our colleagues to be candid, straightforward, and honest. Yet we also want theater, in which we expect everyone to play a part, follow a "script," and deliver their lines properly. The movie producer who expects flattery also wants friendship; the CEO who expects obedience also wants candor; the deal maker who expects victory also wants fairness. Such mixed messages can create tremendous anxiety in organizations because we can find ourselves confused about what is theater and what is not, when to be candid and when to be compliant, who is being honest and who is mouthing lines. And we all get a bit nervous working in such settings because sticking to a script while trying to be genuine is very hard work, indeed.

This is not to say that we don't have roles to play at work, of course. Police officers must project the authority of their position, and doctors must maintain a demeanor of reassurance for their patients. But for mindful leaders, *being comfortable with who we are first* before we shoulder such responsibility is central. For if we actually believe that our celebrity is real or that the title on our business card is who we truly are, we can find ourselves acting out a farce, living in a chat room and doing far more harm than good.

DISSOLVING THE FIXED SENSE OF SELF AND OTHERS

Once our meditation session is over, we naturally go about our daily lives, and for many of us, that means going to work. On occasion, throughout our day, our mindfulness may remind us to slow down, open, and appreciate our circumstances: the flower arrangement on the desk, the young man selling newspapers, the taste of coffee. Over time, dropping our discursiveness and appreciating our lives in the present moment becomes more a way of life than an exceptional experience. Work's ups and downs, life's joy's and disappointments, mundane realities such as having fingers and ironing the clothes—all unfold in the vivid present, and the distinction between mindfulness on and off the cushion gradually dissolves. At the same time, almost to our surprise, we find that we, too, are dissolving. Our fixed sense of who we are and who we need to become gets less urgent, and we discover a very powerful and humbling reality: *we are invisible.*

Of course, we are not talking about literally disappearing and creeping around the office unseen, peeking over the shoulders of our unsuspecting colleagues to see what they are up to. Though this would be a lot of fun, no doubt, the kind of invisibility we gradually discover through mindfulness is something far more practical, indeed: it is how we cultivate humility—a gentle understanding in which we quietly lay down all pretense and open unconditionally to whatever life offers up.

Bernie Glassman Roshi, a colorful and wise American Zen master, teaches his students about this kind of invisible humility with unusual skill. Instead of having his students simply practice sitting meditation in a Zen center, he has them spend periods of time living and practicing on the streets of New York, where they must beg for their food. Lawyers, doctors, business professionals, artists, and the unemployed come together for "street retreats" and live homeless with Roshi, where they humbly discover their invisibility.

> "Street retreats bring us smack against life in all its immediacy," says Roshi. "After just one day on the street people begin to reject you, to deny your existence. When you walk into a restaurant they won't serve you, they won't even let you in. When you ask if you can use the bathroom they say no. People walk away from you because they don't like the way you smell or look."[1]

Spending time homeless on the New York sidewalks is a rough yet effective way to experience this humbling invisibility in which ordinary people don't even notice that we exist. Yet, on the other hand, what Roshi is exposing his students to is a part of our humanity and not all that foreign. We all have a firsthand experience of it as we grow old: fewer and fewer people seem to notice our costumes or hear our message. And as with being homeless on the streets of New York, we notice that as we grow gray, we also grow invisible.

Now, for many of us, such a discovery in our later years or on the streets of New York can be quite discouraging—maybe even shocking. But for mindful leaders, such invisibility comes as no surprise, because it embodies a basic human willingness to be humble—reflecting who we were all along. And rather than being a source of distress, our humility is revealed, through mindfulness meditation, to be a source of inherent comfort because we have fully opened, concealing nothing, and everything is evident. Such total openness reveals not only that have we shed our costumes of self-importance but that there is no place to hang such a costume even if we wished to wear one. Maybe we would like to be perceived as strikingly intelligent or beautiful, or maybe we want the restaurant owner to view us as a powerful, entitled executive. But our mindfulness meditation reveals that such costumes are pointless, and in the tradition of the mindful leader, resting confidently in this invisibility is considered the very essence of humility.

Such humility is not wishy-washy or false modesty, of course. Rather, the fact that we are comfortable being nobody in particular is grounded in the stark realism of mindfulness. Because we have taken the time to befriend ourselves on the cushion, there is no need to make a big deal out of our life story, turning it into theater with its scripts and cues. We need not pretend to be someone else in order to say hello or get the job done. Mindful leaders regard such drama as a lot of useless work. We could be the greatest physicist in the world or a bus driver in Atlanta, Georgia; the president of a major country or a street sweeper in Delhi, India, and if we cultivate the humility of the mindful leader, in a very literal sense, it does not matter what our job or station is—and because it does not matter, doing our job well can then make all the difference in the world. "Whatever you do will be insignificant," said Mahatma Gandhi. "But it is very important that you do it."

THE TALENT OF HUMILITY

Humility, simply put, is the absence of arrogance, which means that we engage our work authentically and communicate with others without self-serving agendas. Such humility means that when we leave our cushion and go to work, we don't buy into the projections or story lines that we lay on ourselves and others. We are willing to set them aside and be naked and invisible—utterly human and open.

Such humility does not require us to keep our heads down and wear drab gray clothing so as not to call attention to ourselves. Quite the opposite. As mindful leaders, humility is how we express our delight—how we appreciate the simple pleasures and great joys. And equally, humility is how we open to life's inconveniences and devastating tragedies. When we are humble, no experience is beneath us, no colleague is unworthy, no moment does not merit our full attention. Because we are humble, we do not pick and choose—savoring only the tasty parts of life and leaving the rest for others. We are willing to experience the entire situation directly and work with every detail.

Ironically, when we are willing to drop *our* pretense, discard *our* costumes, and engage circumstances humbly, we also see others' nakedness as well, which is very organic, raw, and penetrating. To a great degree, all of us don costumes to conceal our vulnerability—to cover up our humanity—and we often do not want to be seen. We feel we have warts of all kinds that should be kept under cover. But for mindful leaders, our humility introduces us to the nakedness of social exchanges. The new sales rep scared to make a mistake, the taxi driver proud of his new cab, the brash creative director overselling her idea, the effective engineer who has every detail nailed down, the gracious business owner, the swaggering lawyer—our humility savors each nuance thoroughly with fresh and unclouded eyes, and everything is evident and appreciated. Such ease of insight and unvarnished discernment have tremendous power and are the basis for communicating authentically.

Dissolving our fixed sense of who we are and in turn appreciating others without their fixed costumes is a profound leadership responsibility that requires a fierce commitment to being free of arrogance. In fact, even the slightest hint of self-importance or charade will cloud the picture and distort the dialogue, so remaining humble is vital if we want to get a clear and realistic picture.

Finally, the talent of humility reminds us of a simple fact of life: each of us, in the final analysis, is alone. We may have friends and loved ones, loyal colleagues and pleasant acquaintances, but the quiet reality is that we wake up each morning alone. We are born alone and we die alone, and we resolve the fundamental questions of life alone, which for mindful leaders is neither bad news nor goods news—just a straight dose of humility.

PART THREE

BRINGING OUR FULL BEING
TO WORK

W HEN WE THINK of living a talented life, we may picture being a fantastic performer or an exciting impresario, or perhaps being virtuous, committing to such ideals as reliability, charity, or justice. For some, living a talented life may even mean denying ourselves certain indulgences or pleasures. Such aspirations are admirable. For mindful leaders, though, living a talented life is not a matter of pursuing an ideal or denying ourselves pleasures. Rather, we live a talented life by first and foremost *being at ease* with who we are and *opening* to whatever circumstances we face.

Such comfort arises gradually out of our mindfulness practice, and over time, almost magically, we discover that we are bringing our full being to work and living a life naturally endowed with the talents that we have aspired to all along. The more at ease we are with ourselves, the more we open respectfully to our world and engage difficulties patiently and without resentment. The less we struggle to become someone else, the more enthusiastic we are being ourselves and taking a larger view of life. The more we drop our discursiveness and open to life on its terms, the more we discover the ease of simplicity and humility. For mindful leaders, then, the core of leadership springs from being at ease and opening, and such qualities inform everything we do and say and accomplish.

Because such comfort emerges from the mindfulness practice, it is not a matter of speculation or wishful thinking but is very explicit and tangible. The talents we cultivate on the cushion unfold in everyday life as a definite and unmistakable experience in which we are fully present and astutely available to our world, and such presence is expressed when we "synchronize."

14

SYNCHRONIZING

MANY OF US live our lives as if we were running a three-ring circus: we take center stage as "ring-leaders" and try to manage our lives as a performance or project, keeping events on track and on schedule and preventing all kinds of problems. Essentially, this ringleader is what we call our mind, which we generally regard as being located from our neck up. Although our mind is shapeless, it is nonetheless a very familiar presence because we spend a lot of time conversing with ourselves. In this respect, our mind is like our best friend—someone always available to talk to and commiserate with. But our mind is also like a ringleader because we often find ourselves struggling to maintain order in a life that is always verging slightly out of control—trying to make sense of the whole experience and make our lives behave.

The first ring of our metaphorical circus is our emotions, which are like unruly but beautiful creatures that we work hard to tame. We want our emotions to behave themselves, but they are always unpredictable. Some emotions seem very powerful and threatening, so we have to keep them caged for fear that they will escape and make us do all kinds of things that we might regret. On occasion, an emotion may break out and frighten others or we may let one out of its cage to prance around and have a little naughty fun, but generally, we work hard to keep them under lock and key. Other emotions we domesticate, and they behave like circus monkeys—entertaining us and keeping us distracted and happy. Of course, even circus monkeys can get out of hand, causing quarrels and mishaps. If everything goes well, however, our emotions behave themselves and perform on cue, and the ringleader feels in control and satisfied.

The second ring of the circus is our body, which often seems to be going along and cooperating quite nicely but then suddenly poses problems—sometimes small problems, such as stubbing our toe or having a pimple blossom on the tip of our nose; other times big problems, such as becoming paralyzed or developing a life-threatening disease. Of course, there is the problem of growing old, in which our body gradually seems to stop cooperating and all kinds of difficulties appear. Generally, our ringleader tries to get our body to oblige. Maybe we work out at the gym or eat properly so as to keep in shape. Other times, though, we dress up to have fun and stay out late partying, and the next morning our body refuses to cooperate at all. Like our emotions, our physical presence can be cooperative or unruly, and the ringleader works hard to make our body behave itself.

The third ring of our circus is the audience—the phenomenal world that surrounds us. This rich display is at once amazing and terrifying, pleasurable and painful, playful and rude. There are trees and cars, neighbors and newborns, wars and lovers. There are bills to pay, vacations to take, parents to love, and children to care for. For the most part, we find our place in this vast display, savoring what we prefer, avoiding as much difficulty as possible, and exploring the wonder of it all when we have the time and inclination. If everything goes well, our world applauds on cue and we are happy because we are all enjoying the circus we call "our life."

This three-ring circus may be quite familiar to many of us, but when we practice mindfulness meditation, we gradually learn that such an existential arrangement with our lives is highly questionable. In fact, mindfulness reveals that our three-ring circus is simply theater substituting for reality, and we begin asking ourselves some very basic questions: How is it that we have come to experience our life as a conversation with ourselves? Who is this voice inside our head, and who's talking to whom? What is this "audience" that keeps showing up, and how is it that we are simultaneously both ringleader and audience?

When we practice mindfulness meditation, we discover in very tangible terms that our circuslike arrangement with life is not only suspect but is also masking a profound and touching reality: *who, what, and where we are functions as one vast synchronized moment*—our arrangement with life is a singular event rather than a set of uncooperative and often threatening forces. Our mind, emotions, body, and the phenomenal world are not a three-ring circus but a unified sensual experience so razor-sharp that recognizing the experience for what it is wakes us up to an entirely different way of leading our lives.

Now, discovering that we are synchronized need not be a big deal. In fact, it is our natural state of mind and is more familiar than we might think. Throughout our lives, we synchronize hundreds of times a day, but we often speed past such moments, anxious to keep our circus in order. When the phone rings, for example, we suddenly synchronize: mind, body, emotions, and phenomenal world functioning as a singular moment. But almost instantaneously, we panic a bit and decide to *manage* the experience rather than *live* it, and the phone call becomes part of the audience and we a ringleader. We find ourselves synchronized while playing sports, nursing our child, rescuing a dying friend, or simply smelling a flower. Mindfulness meditation awakens us to these experiences, permitting us to slow down, drop the panic, and savor the fact that we are synchronized in the present moment.

On the other hand, when we commit to being synchronized, we discover that some of our most basic assumptions about life and our world are just plain inaccurate. We find that, unsynchronized, we become victims of our schemes to manage our lives; but, synchronized, the very same circumstances offer opportunity for extraordinary accomplishment. For example, we typically think that "intelligence" is a function of being "animate," or alive. Humans and dogs, horses and crows, even ants and small fish have varying levels of intelligence. But rocks and trees, oceans and asteroids are inanimate, and not being alive, they don't have intelligence. When we synchronize in the present moment, this whole approach to intelligence "flips," for we see quite directly that the line between intelligent life and seemingly inanimate objects blurs. Where is the intelligence when we taste a piece of cantaloupe? Is it in the tongue or the fruit? Where is the intelligence in smelling a magnolia—in the nose or the flower? When we synchronize, we discover that intelligence lies not with a ringleader but with the arising of a fully harmonized moment. Intelligence is the fact that a tongue and a piece of fruit appear at the same place and at the same time, not something located between our ears. When we synchronize, we discover that intelligence has no location but is like space, informing and invigorating everything.

When we synchronize, we also discover a new set of rules for leading our lives. For example, we are all familiar with the seasons: winter, spring, summer, and fall. Each season has its own poetry and texture. Each makes demands and offers pleasures. And each somehow leads to the next. We know that the four seasons happen over a period of about 365 days and they are caused by the Earth going around the sun. When we synchronize with our world, however, the four seasons are no longer just a 365-day weather cycle but instead are recognized as woven into everything, everywhere, all the time. A human life or a business project, an evening meal or a savings account, a love affair or a pair of glasses—all unfold as seasons. Wanting our bank accounts and love lives to be in a perpetual state of spring, for example, becomes pointless when we are synchronized. Expecting financial investments to yield a steady return would be comparable to expecting an apple tree to offer ripe fruit twenty-four hours a day, seven days a week. When we commit to being synchronized in our life, we no longer struggle against life's rules but understand that we are inherently a product of them.

Most important, when we synchronize, we naturally express the talents of a mindful leader. Rather than living our lives as a three-ring circus, we live fully engaged and open in the present moment. We begin to understand that being humble, patient, and wise is not a matter of trying to be a good girl or boy but a matter of committing to who we are—synchronized with all that is arising. And it is from here, fully synchronized as mindful leaders, that we understand how to genuinely contribute to our world.

15

ENGAGING THE WHOLE

W HEN WE ARE NOT synchronized, the rules for
living our lives are crudely straightforward:
"Focus on desired results and achieve them as
quickly as possible." "Amass valuable possessions and avoid
unpleasant experiences." "Protect yourself unless there is a reason not to." There are many more unspoken but familiar rules
that we use to give ourselves a false sense of control, and unraveling such self-deception is a central challenge for mindful leaders. When we synchronize, however, we discover that these
rules no longer apply—in fact, they never worked to begin
with—and we perceive an entirely different relationship to life.
A shift occurs, in which we engage life not as a three-ring circus but as a "whole"—a singular, intact reality.

Engaging "reality" can sound both profound and ridiculously obvious at the same time. Putting our socks on, driving
to work, shaking hands with a colleague, are all quite real. Making a big existential deal out of such mundane experiences
seems a bit silly. Yet, if we examine carefully, synchronizing
with our world introduces the possibility that such seemingly
small gestures may have a greater impact on our world than
we would "think." Maybe we are so integrated into the func-
tional fabric of this unified whole that our daily behaviors can

have far-reaching effects throughout organizations, families, neighborhoods, and beyond. Let's consider a simple example. On a recent visit to Boulder, Colorado, I spent an evening with two good friends sharing an excellent meal, a few glasses of wine, and an intimate conversation. We ended the evening late, and I strolled lazily back to my hotel. Now, one of the distinctive beauties of Boulder is the foothills that rise in noble silence above the town, and I noticed that generous, wide benches had been placed along the streets facing the shallow peaks. It was the dead of night, the streets were empty, and I decided to take a seat and quietly savor the moment. The circumstances easily shifted into their natural totality, and I simply relaxed, appreciating the good fortune. Yet, after a few minutes and seemingly out of nowhere, a shiny, clean bus pulled up to my bench, opened its door, and a young man smiled and said, "Hello. Waiting for the bus?" I smiled back, a bit surprised, and said, "No, I'm just sitting here enjoying the moment, but thanks." "Have a good night," he replied, then closed the door and drove slowly away. For me at that moment, the bus showing up was just as impressive as the mountains, sky, and earth showing up. Just as there was a larger synchronized whole unfolding between myself and the foothills, there was an equally inspiring harmony in my short exchange with the bus driver.

Now, for any city dweller, having a bus pause and open its doors is pretty familiar territory. Sit at a bus stop, and sure enough, a bus will eventually, well, stop. But when we are synchronized, we intuitively appreciate that a lot more is going on than just a mere transaction between "me" and the "bus" and the "bus stop." At 2:00 A.M., in the middle of Boulder, among the foothills of the Rockies, all I had to do was *sit down*—the most inconsequential and ordinary of gestures—and an entire system responded. Dozens of buses, hundreds of city employees, thousands of miles of roads, work schedules, gas stations, traffic lights, and repair depots all showed up, synchronized in a simple gesture of a bus stopping and two human beings saying hello. I had paused to appreciate the Rockies and, almost mistakenly, invited the "whole" of Boulder, Colorado's transportation system to respond.

Now, any economist understands that systems such as public transit are a marvel to behold. But for mindful leaders, to synchronize with such marvels—be they transit systems or mountain ranges—is not an intellectual exercise but an instinctive, physical immediacy that offers fresh and powerful options for productively engaging the world. When we synchronize with our experience as a whole, our behaviors, great and small, become as much an *expression of* the system as a *reaction to* it. We live fully integrated with our circumstances, and our "presence" is how the situation adapts and expresses its intelligence. Consider the following brief story.

Many hundreds of years ago along the banks of the Yellow River in ancient China, a small village sprang up called Lu Chow. Here at Lu Chow, the riverbanks narrowed and the waters deepened, affording an opportunity for transporting goods and livestock across the river. A vibrant ferry service grew and with it the village. Lodging, tearooms, a blacksmith, a dry goods store, and even a school found footing, and the village prospered. The villagers knew that their prosperity came from the ferry and its many customers, so they kept a caring eye on the comings and goings.

One day, a young child came running into the village screaming, "Come quickly, come quickly. The ferry has capsized and people are drowning. Help! Help!" And, sure enough, all the villagers dropped what they were doing and raced down to the ferry to lend a hand—except for the blacksmith. Instead of heading for the ferry, he ran in the opposite direction. People stopped and grumbled, "Now we know who to depend on when things go wrong. Look at that cowardly blacksmith scurrying away when he is most needed."

As people rushed to the capsized ferry, they struggled valiantly to save those in the water, but they were too late. Those who had fallen into the river had been pulled downstream by the strong current, and the villagers could see people struggling in the rapids as they were swept out of sight around the bend. No one could see the blacksmith, however, just past the curve of the river extending a bamboo pole to those in need, pulling them to shore one by one.

Unlike the well-intentioned villagers, the blacksmith "engaged the whole": his behaviors were as much an expression of the circumstances as they were a reaction to them. He knew that "results"—saving the drowning passengers—were inherently defined by the river, terrain, and timing, not by his personal need to help. Going downstream rather than rushing in panic to the scene of the disaster was a choice that followed the contours of his world; because he was synchronized, he was skillfully in tune with the facts, and his presence was, in many respects, an expression of the situation's intelligence.

Like the blacksmith, mindful leaders engage the whole and discover a new organic approach to leading and understanding organizations. Rather than jumping to conclusions or pushing for business results, we perceive a full picture that guides our behavior and tempers our views. Ordinary moments such as greeting the UPS deliveryman in his shiny, clean brown truck or listening to an attorney offer exclusively positive views of her client's behavior reveal much larger truths. Like the blacksmith, we intuitively understand where things are going, when we witness the discipline of a UPS driver; we know the endgame when we hear a one-sided legal pitch that strains to sugarcoat the facts. Larger moments such as producing 150,000 new cars and trucks across Southeast Asia or enacting immigration policy in developed countries reveal the whole, and like the blacksmith, we know where things are going, in terms of all the potential environmental, social, political, and economic consequences.

When we synchronize with our environment, issues of timing become obvious: there is no need to resolve a conflict in the midst of a heated argument or introduce an innovation while markets are confused. We arrive at the right place at the right time with the right resources because we are not intent on *our* agenda but understand that agendas are an expression of circumstances. Likewise, we do not mistakenly take insults or compliments at face value. Instead, arrogance, deception, impoverishment, and flattery become windows into their authors' mind-set rather than smoke screens that can confuse or intimidate us. And as with our blacksmith, resistance and chaos are not just obstacles but, equally important, an invitation to cleverly yield.

Most important, by engaging the whole, mindful leaders recognize that personally living a sane and dignified life is inherently tied to the totality of human society. An old Tibetan proverb reminds us, "Instead of putting leather over the entire planet, first put your shoes on." Wishing others to be wise and respectful and our workplace to be accommodating and uplifting without first cultivating these qualities within ourselves is like trying to cover the world in leather so that we can walk around barefoot. When we are synchronized, we understand that such an approach is unrealistic and arrogant. Rather, engaging the whole commits us to cultivating our natural talents and sanity as *the* first, vital step in cultivating a dignified workplace—indeed, in fostering a dignified world.

16

INSPIRING HEALTH AND WELL-BEING IN ORGANIZATIONS

THROUGHOUT my twenty-five-year corporate career, I have always been fascinated by the disconnect between most organizations and their employees regarding health and well-being. A routine question I often ask employees is, "Does the organization you work for care about your health and well-being and that of your family?" Typically, most answer "no," and some even believe that the organization is deliberately uncaring. Now, the irony is that all the organizations in which I asked this question were spending huge sums to provide their employees with health and well-being services: medical and dental care, employee assistance programs, subsidized physicals and health screenings, cigarette smoking cessation programs, stress reduction seminars, paid sick time, vacation days, and much, much more. For some reason, the financial commitment to health and well-being that these organizations were making was getting lost in translation when it came to inspiring appreciation and loyalty from employees. Such a senseless disconnect, with all its attendant misunderstandings and problems, is unnecessary.

For mindful leaders, cultivating health and well-being within organizations is not a choice, nor does it reflect a mere willingness to incur a cost. It's not as if the well-being of employees were a nice frill that we could bargain away or hedge on a bit. Rather, for mindful leaders, inspiring health and well-being in organizations is how we engage the whole and commit to what is basically sane and obvious—like committing to stringent accounting discipline or to the safety of children. It is indispensable, realistic management, which requires crafting and implementing strategy that demonstrates genuine commitment to employees' well-being and inviting a reciprocal commitment in return.

This is not to say, of course, that fostering health and well-being only involves managing benefits policies. Ask any ecologist, military strategist, or urban planner, and he or she will be the first to say that all organizations function as a living organism, requiring care, planning, and holistic thinking to keep them healthy. But for mindful leaders, such a holistic approach is not simply a way to *think* about organizations but is also how we *behave* when we are open, synchronized, and in tune with our circumstances.

As mindful leaders, we inspire health and well-being in organizations from precisely such a perspective: naturally open to a large view yet in tune with the contours of our world. It's like seeing a city from an airplane flying twenty thousand feet above its tallest building and simultaneously sorting out a traffic jam at Fifteenth and Market Streets. When we engage organizations from such a perspective, we discover that leading is about cultivating health, not just achieving success; encouraging precision and care, not just avoiding problems; inspiring well-being throughout the whole organization, not just driving for results.

Typically, we lead organizations in a linear fashion—trying

to get somewhere and meet or exceed goals. When we are synchronized with work, however, we discover that such a linear approach, while necessary, is insufficient if we want to truly "succeed." As mindful leaders, we understand that getting from point A to point B requires that we never carelessly neglect where we are, and by attending mindfully to our organizational setting *as we succeed,* we discover how to be sane and dignified in a workplace that too often demeans and abuses.

Much has been written about what makes an organization healthy: creative freedom, candor and courage, excellent vision, properly distributed resources, disciplined processes, exceptional management, and much more. The list is long. For mindful leaders, cultivating such organizational health requires first and foremost a mastery of organizational conduct—a fluency in nine basic competencies:

1. Eliminate toxicity.
2. Appreciate health.
3. Build trust.
4. Send clear messages.
5. Embrace resistance.
6. Understand blindness.
7. Accept invitations.
8. Heal wounds.
9. Be realistic.

ELIMINATE TOXICITY

Organizations generally do not tolerate sexual harassment, racial discrimination, fraud, and physical violence. Such egregiously "toxic" acts have no place at work. Yet abusive language, unreasonable demands, arrogant remarks, and greed are just a few of the many toxic behaviors that are tolerated—at times, even celebrated—in the workplace. For mindful leaders, inspiring health and well-being requires that we place the highest priority on understanding the full range of toxicity and eliminating it from the workplace. This is not to say that we must create a "toxic police force" to hunt down offenders. Nor should we ever expect to definitively eliminate all toxic difficulties from organizations. Rather, as mindful leaders, we viscerally understand the crippling effect toxicity has on organizations—how it instills fear and anxiety into decision making and demoralizes employees. And because we never neglect our present circumstances, we are willing to do the work of a "toxin handler," a role so aptly described by Peter Frost, in his book *Toxic Emotions at Work:*

> The work of toxin handlers . . . is complex, subtle and demanding. It is a necessary and often inevitable part of the healthy functioning organization. A whole repertoire of skills and competences—listening, holding space for healing, buffering pain, extricating people from painful situations, transforming pain— is employed in toxin handling. When these skills are executed well, they can help people who are suffering to better cope with painful situations. The use of these skills can prevent toxins from flooding the workplace. . . . Simply knowing that someone has this role can have a calming effect for others in the organization.[1]

APPRECIATE HEALTH

When we are dead set on achieving success, we can view our work through lenses that distort the whole picture. And the greatest distortion of all is taking the organization's health for granted. This is not to say, of course, that we should not pursue success with a sense of urgency and focus. The problem is being blinded by such efforts and in turn neglecting where we are. We've seen the results of such blind ambition: safety suffers; greed flourishes; harsh, demeaning language weakens dialogue; and creativity is undermined. Mindful leaders avoid such pitfalls by appreciating health.

In all organizations, much happens every day that is amazing. Paychecks for thousands of employees are cut accurately; complex technology functions seamlessly; sales personnel successfully interact with millions of customers; products are shipped and received on time. When we synchronize with an organization, we never take such health for granted but instead openly and regularly appreciate it. This is not to say that we must orchestrate contrived occasions to recognize others' contributions. For mindful leaders, thanking others, inspecting successful results, and recognizing contributions all come naturally because such appreciation of organizational health arises from our openness and awareness. In a sense, pursuing success without appreciating the whole organization along the way is impossible, since the synchronized mind is constantly curious and unwilling to take anything for granted.

BUILD TRUST

Inspiring health and well-being in organizations requires us to be realistic about what is and is not trustworthy. Such insight does not involve wishful thinking—*hoping* that our employer will be nice to us and keep us secure; nor does it involve taking matters for granted—simply *assuming* that people will follow through, keep to their word, and treat one another decently. Rather, for mindful leaders, trust involves having a *firm, realistic conviction* about who and what are reliable and in turn fostering such trust and conviction in the entire organization. When we are realistically open to our work setting, we know who is honest and who is not; we know the difference between a well-tailored story and the truth. We can tell who is worthy of our confidence and who is apt to shirk accountability. As mindful leaders, we are naturally alert to who and what can be trusted, and we respect such trustworthiness, seeking to strengthen it throughout the organization.

The opposite of such trust is hypocrisy and betrayal, with leaders pretending to be accountable but secretly preferring expediency—which is a potent poison, indeed. As Peter Frost observes in *Toxic Emotions at Work:*

> Perhaps nothing creates . . . people's emotional pain more surely than feeling that psychological or emotional contracts they have with organizations have been betrayed. We've all seen cases where people who have been treated unfairly withdraw their effort, refusing to do their work beyond their job descriptions or assist coworkers. On the other hand, organizations that

promote trust and a sense of fair play reduce the likelihood of emotional toxicity among their employees.[2]

For mindful leaders, strengthening trust requires that we
know how and when to confidently rely on colleagues and
respect the work they deliver day in and day out. Yet, in the
final analysis, nothing is totally reliable, and because of that,
nothing is ever taken for granted.

SEND CLEAR MESSAGES

Sending unambiguous messages within organizations is not as
easy as we often think. For example, salary increases are probably one of the most common signals we receive and send in
organizations, but they are often executed in ways that create
more confusion than clarity. A misstep that I have seen hundreds of times is turning a reward into a punishment. An
employee who has performed admirably and exceeded expectations has been told to expect a handsome increase. But the
manager forgets to submit the paperwork on time, and the
employee is left simmering and resentful that a promise was
broken. When the increase is finally processed, with all the
attendant apologies, the employee is left with a sense of having been mistreated, not rewarded.

Unfortunately, such blunders are all too frequent in organizations. Have you ever waited in a reception area ornamented
with an arrangement of wilted flowers? Or how does it feel to
read in your organization's annual report that the senior management team has been awarded millions of dollars in bonuses
during a year when hundreds of employees were laid off? In

such circumstances we pick up an unsettling hidden message that seems to define the situation as a whole.

Mindful leaders can avoid such reckless and unnecessary missteps by truly committing to the organization's health and well-being. Organizations send hundreds of messages to thousands of people each day through reception areas, annual reports, customer service contact, advertising, business meetings, and much more. And we all know how it feels when genuine communication takes place—when we feel listened to and appreciated as customers or employees and receive genuine, unmistakable messages. I continue to marvel, for example, at the discipline and professionalism exhibited in well-managed hospital settings where doctors and nurses patiently discuss medical procedures with family members. Or how companies such as UPS, Starbucks, and Harry & David's send the firm and unambiguous message that excellent, reliable service will never—*never*—be compromised. For the mindful leader, such clear communication is a vital sign of an organization committed not just to the bottom line but to the health and well-being of everyone involved.

EMBRACE RESISTANCE

No matter where we find ourselves, there will always be someone resisting something. Such resistance can range from minor confrontations over who gets a printer in their office to monumental struggles over who gets to own the company. Typically, if we are just trying to accomplish something, we tend to dismiss such resistance as a nuisance or mere speed bump. But when we attend mindfully to present circumstances, we appreciate resistance as the expected outcome when the status quo meets the future and opposition naturally arises. Fully appreciating where, how, and why organizational resistance arises and sustains itself is of the utmost importance for mindful leaders because, unattended, such resistance can inflate simple problems into unnecessary disasters, with all the resulting toxicity.

I recall an assignment in which a company was laying off about fifty employees and management had come to a bitter impasse over how to proceed. The customer service and order-entry functions were to be merged, and some departments were going to suffer greater losses than others. Despite the availability of severance packages to be offered to those laid off, none of the managers was willing to sacrifice a thing. Arguments, threats, and slammed doors were the order of the day—with a festering whiff of potential lawsuits lingering in the air. I was asked to attend a meeting and help the four managers responsible for executing the reorganization to reach a resolution. After listening to the tense reasoning and conflicting viewpoints, I posed this question: "If you had to guess, how many people in each of your organizations would want to be laid off and receive the proposed severance package?" I asked each manager to take a moment to reflect and just give me a rough number—a guesstimate. Sure enough, each manager estimated that somewhere between 40 and 60 percent of his employees would welcome being released—a point of remarkable agreement, given all the conflict. By engaging resistance at the right time with the right question, we found that the goal of laying off fifty employees was quite achievable—the challenge was preserving the health and well-being of the organization in the process.

For mindful leaders, then, there is no need to avoid or sug-arcoat conflict; such resistance merely reflects the natural functioning of an organization. The key is having a synchronized understanding of when and how to lend a hand, which requires genuine interest, timing, and skill.

UNDERSTAND BLINDNESS

Despite all the shortcomings of former U.S. Secretary of Defense Donald Rumsfeld, he nonetheless occasionally offered sound advice, albeit at times convoluted and quirky:

> There are known knowns; there are things we know we know. We also know there are known unknowns; that is to say, we know there are some things we do not know. But there are also unknown unknowns—the ones we don't know we don't know . . .[3]

For mindful leaders, such a poetically strained reminder is not as bizarre as it appears but is an ever present aspect of living a synchronized life. When we pursue objectives, we tend to eliminate or disregard information and experiences that *seem* either irrelevant or unhelpful to getting the job done—which, on the surface, makes sense. However, such elimination, especially if it is done recklessly or out of frustration, creates blind spots that can derail even the best plans. When we synchronize, however, we intuitively know that our circumstances are uncertain; in fact, we are viscerally confident that there is always something we are missing, and such attentiveness makes us astutely aware of our surroundings—seeking clarity, inviting feedback, listening to criticism, considering new angles. Such awareness is not hesitant paranoia but a flexibility of mind that is more poetic than mechanical, more willing than rigid, more receptive than out of touch. By permitting ourselves to remain alert and not be distracted by the demands of feverishly pursuing achievement, we avoid being blindsided by speeding past vital issues and problems that need our attention. And given where history has arrived, maybe Secretary Rumsfeld should have taken his own advice a bit more to heart.

ACCEPT INVITATIONS

Organizations are constantly inviting our involvement—to solve problems, to celebrate successes, to contribute resources, to purchase goods and services. And on the surface, most invitations can seem appealing and worthy of our attention. For mindful leaders, accepting invitations in organizations requires balance, wisdom, and a dash of skepticism.

We all know what it's like to answer our phone only to find ourselves listening to a pitch encouraging us to contribute our money to some cause. We can feel trapped at times by such invitations. On the other hand, we may notice that a colleague is having a problem framing a legal policy with which we have extensive experience, for example, and offering our opinion seems natural and appropriate. For mindful leaders, knowing which invitation to accept or reject and which to offer our resources to is basic. But more important, knowing how to discern a vital invitation that could easily be overlooked requires a synchronized openness to circumstances.

I recall working with a publishing executive who ran a midsize software company in California. Every month, he and his colleagues would attend an operations review and report solid results to their corporate headquarters in New York. New software releases were on time, sales budgets were met, and profit margins were firm. Since I sat on the executive committee in New York, I had the vantage point of simply listening and appreciating the results. But there was something at the end of each monthly meeting that disturbed me a bit. After the CEO and corporate finance people got their questions answered, there was a moment when the software company's president would launch into a seemingly circular discussion of culture and communications and how he placed the utmost emphasis on such things. To all outward appearances, his speeches seemed routine and a bit rambling, and most people in the room were scarcely interested. For me, however, the rambling seemed more like an invitation than a lullaby.

After investigating further and making a trip out to spend some time with the team, I found that many of the senior managers felt slighted and misunderstood by corporate headquarters. In fact, they had heard rumors that we intended to sell them in the next month or two and, despite all our denials, were convinced that we were about to jettison them from the team. Many had their résumés out on the street, and rumors were spiraling out of control. The president needed our help to stabilize the situation, and his way of inviting such help had been camouflaged in those meandering remarks on the importance of managing culture and communications.

For mindful leaders, fostering health and well-being in organizations requires an astute alertness to how people ask for help. Some find it easy; others struggle. Some shift their burdens inappropriately, and others shoulder too much. The challenge is to be in tune with our workplace so we can recognize and accept the invitations that need our attention.

HEAL WOUNDS

When we think of healing, what typically comes to mind is hospital care or maybe a simple bandage on the knee. Or maybe we think of relationships in which we permit hurt feelings to mend and grow healthy again. In work settings, healing is not typically considered a core competency for leaders—unless, of course, we value health and well-being as a fundamental priority. As Peter Frost observes in *Toxic Emotions at Work*, leaders who heal

> respond compassionately to pain in their organizations in order to either minimize or prevent it, to identify it, contain it, remove it or find ways for people to live with it constructively. Their compassion takes the form of noticing and feeling the pain of someone else and then acting in a way that is intended to help the other person heal. . . . They are not only caregivers who help heal people who hurt; they are also leaders who work with pain in ways that are designed to sustain and enhance performance in the workplace.[4]

We have all seen such healing at work: a lawyer clearing the air by offering a concession in a bruising negotiation, a stressed-out manager apologizing to a colleague for a thoughtless remark, a nurse thanking a patient for her patience. For mindful leaders, such seemingly small healing gestures have tremendous power to sustain a healthy, thriving workplace because they infuse and inform the whole organization.

I recall being part of a bank's company-wide "Customer Service Improvement Program," in which all employees were required to learn new systems, meet rigorous quality standards, and offer a more responsive level of service. A lot of pressure was on to adapt and learn new skills. Colleagues were being transferred and laid off; ambitious new managers were pushing relentlessly toward stretch goals. Late nights, long hours, and fierce demands were the order of the day, and many people were wilting from exhaustion.

Cheerleading meetings, contests, and recognition programs had little impact. Employees dismissed such efforts as placebos, which offered no genuine acknowledgment of their distress.

Then one day, during a weekly quality control briefing, Jerry, an old-school manager who had been with the firm for twenty years, said, "I want to do something that is just plain ridiculous and I don't know how it's going to come off, but somehow I think it makes sense right now. We've tried a lot of things to help people through these tough times, but let me explain what I want to do." Sure enough, two days later, we found Jerry dressed up as a pink rabbit, walking around the operations floors stopping at people's desks to ask, "How's it goin'?" and to thank people for their efforts. People were shocked, tickled, and enthused to see a pink rabbit sitting among employees, dispensing "Dinner for Two" gift cards, and expressing appreciation for their hard work. And while such antics did invite a few cynical remarks and were but one piece of a larger strategy, employees reminisced often and cheerfully about "the week the bunny visited" to say thanks. A small dose of playful theater injected into a high-pressure environment created the healing humor and collegiality needed to regain some lost momentum.

Of course, healing pain in organizations is seldom as much fun as dressing up as a pink rabbit, but it almost always involves a sense of relief that can inform and strengthen organizations. In the end, healing organizational wounds takes skill and timing and often courage because applying the medicine requires vulnerability. For the mindful leader, such skill comes from the confidence of being synchronized with the fragile points in organizations and feeling directly the need for health and healing.

BE REALISTIC

A colleague who holds positions on several boards of directors asked me one day, "Why do I always seem to bump into difficulties on my board assignments? It seems as if I'm always in some kind of battle." Knowing my friend's idealism and passion quite well, I responded immediately, "Because when you encounter hypocrisy, you feel justified in confronting it." And herein lies one of the most subtle traps of leadership—placing idealism ahead of realism, seeking to create a great and decent world without first skillfully working with the world that we have inherited.

When we candidly take stock of the workplace, we discover that it is like a river—never static, fraught with all kinds of contradictions, delights, successes, and misdirected intentions. And, as with a river, sometimes work flows evenly and people cooperate and understand one another; other times the flow is erratic or chaotic and people conflict and misunderstand one another. "Idealists" would have us eliminate all the missteps, toxicity, and conflicts, thereby permitting the organization to flow naturally and evenly forward. "Realists," on the other hand, respect the momentum—whether smooth, rocky, delightful, or distasteful.

On one of my assignments, I was asked to help a management team revitalize its demoralized workforce. Spread out across the country, the business had grown through a series of small acquisitions until it had reached "critical mass." Human resources policies, internal communications, hiring practices, and more needed to be standardized and radically improved. For me and the managers involved, the mission was a real pleasure, since the thousand plus employees appreciated the more coordinated professional approach. However, while all these optimistic efforts unfolded, a lingering reality continued to define the company's tone and culture: *venture capitalists owned the business, and their focus was exclusively on short-term profits and personal gain.* While management worked hard to send a message of professionalism, fairness, and respect, the financial administrators issued harsh, arrogant, and self-serving messages designed to maximize income for investors. "Ideally," the financial types would have taken a course or two in "emotional intelligence" and learned to run the organization as a business rather than a personal wealth-generating machine. But "realistically," such a possibility was unlikely, indeed.

The idealists would begin each day speculating about the probability of the glorified bean counters' growing up and permitting people to manage the company as a real enterprise. And inevitably, such hopes would be dashed by the unfolding of yet another shortsighted financial decision: bonuses would be paid to the bankers but denied to others; investments in the business would be reduced, but corporate overhead would grow; profits would be drained to pay for debt management, and sales targets would be set ridiculously high. For the idealists, such hypocrisy was viscerally offensive, and daily work became disheartening.

The realists, on the other hand, were preparing to be sold. They knew that milking a healthy business to death was absurd and it was only a matter of time before experienced, capable management would take over. Who, when, and how they did not know, but they respected the momentum of where things were going. Fighting the bankers' greed was a waste of time and productive energy; finding a buyer for the company was not. In essence, the realists saw where the momentum was headed, and they took the lead in finding a buyer and helped arrange the successful sale of the business to a company interested in growth rather than exploitation. Instead of fighting the tastelessness, arrogance, and greed, the realists paddled *with* the current, taking advantage of the momentum and accelerating an inevitable sale rather than waiting for it to happen.

When we synchronize with our workplace, we realize, like our realists, that our circumstances represent a fluid blend of shifting dynamics. Political priorities, available resources, commitments, past decisions, and blind spots are among the many things that are reflected in a single moment, and we can call such moments a success, problem, conflict, job well done, or crisis. For mindful leaders, such moments are part of a flow rather than a static idealistic event, and knowing how to "paddle with" the fluid momentum of organizations requires a synchronized sense of timing, awareness, and realism.

17

ESTABLISHING AUTHENTICITY

MUCH IS WRITTEN in today's business literature about what makes a leader authentic. Some experts speak of having strong conviction and "knowing oneself"; others speak of "walking the talk" and "having many faces for many people." Much of the research being done offers practical insights and useful advice. For mindful leaders, however, cultivating our authenticity springs directly from our willingness to open and synchronize with the present moment—which, ironically, both simplifies and expands our challenge.

Traditionally, authenticity is said to be cultivated on both the outer and inner levels. Cultivating outer authenticity is quite straightforward. If we treat people decently, over time such good actions become part of how we behave, and we are relied on and appreciated as decent or authentic persons. If, on the other hand, we say pleasant and appealing things but then do and say the opposite behind closed doors, people reject us as fake and inauthentic hypocrites. Cultivating outer authenticity is actually fairly simple—though at times very demanding. If we pause for a moment and consider our lives, we all know what is decent and wholesome. We know how to respect others and how to be generous and helpful. Such decency is very natural and uncomplicated, and cultivating this outer authenticity requires that we follow this instinct under all circumstances.

Inner authenticity, however, is not just being a good person in the conventional sense. Inner authenticity is a primordial confidence—an unshakable enthusiasm—that naturally arises when we are synchronized. Free from fear, arrogance, and greed, naturally expressing the talents that arise out of simply existing, we discover that being at ease with ourselves is *powerful*. Traditionally, a person who possesses this primordial confidence is said to manifest *wangthang,* or a "field of power."

It is quite difficult—maybe even impossible—to describe a person who exhibits the power of wangthang, though when you meet such a person, it is disturbingly obvious. And in this case, we are not talking about personal magnetism, such as meeting a smiling overpolished politician or a perfectly sculpted movie star. When it comes to experiencing a person who exhibits wangthang, it's like meeting a carefree breeze embodied in stone—a pervasive sense of refreshing openness that is utterly indestructible. Needless to say, it's always best to meet such a person face-to-face rather than rely on descriptions.

Throughout my thirty years of Buddhist training, I have had the good fortune to study with Tibetan Buddhist masters who radiate wangthang, one of whom was His Holiness the Sixteenth Karmapa, the head of the Kagyu school of Tibetan Buddhism. In the late 1970s, I was attending H.H. Karmapa for several days during a trip to upstate New York, where he was to perform initiations and ceremonies for a Chinese Buddhist community. On the one hand, there was nothing special about the trip. Roughly a dozen people accompanied his holiness— translators, monks, cooks, and security personnel. We drove through the New York countryside, stayed at a wonderful farmhouse, and hundreds of people attended His Holiness's ceremony. On the other hand, the atmosphere around His Holiness involved everyone in an unfolding yet continuous moment that was vast, magical, and unusually penetrating. On one occasion, for example, several of us were accompanying His Holiness on a stroll in the woods when a small sparrow suddenly landed at His Holiness's feet—only slightly unusual, given the setting. What was so penetrating was the equally sudden and utterly uncontrived joy that flowed from His Holiness upon engaging such a superb little creature. His delight and playfulness—he stooped down and seemed to have a conversation with the small bird and actually reached his hand out to within inches of the bird's beak—was so pure and simple, and the smile on his face so clean and natural, that I and others were drawn into a sense of complete relief: a freedom filled with finality and depth that was profoundly engaging. His Holiness naturally radiated wangthang—a field of powerful authenticity that by its very nature inspired, uplifted, and challenged all those in his company.

Of course, establishing such inner authenticity is not some kind of religious chauvinism, as if only great spiritual leaders such as the karmapa can be authentic and the rest of us must fake it. Establishing our inner authenticity is entirely human and is not far-fetched or unattainable. Nor is it a one-shot deal, in which either we suddenly become a great enlightened being or we give up, pop open another beer, and watch television.

Wangthang is established by opening our heart to the world around us—letting go of our insecurities and resentments and bravely permitting our world to touch us—and this can be done by anyone, anywhere, anytime. In the tradition of the mindful leader, establishing this inner authenticity is essential for leading others and for living a dignified and uplifted life.

THE FOUR MARKS OF A MINDFUL LEADER

Establishing wangthang is both simple and difficult. As human beings, this inner authenticity is actually with us all the time and pervades everything we do. But, unfortunately, we spend a tremendous amount of emotional and spiritual time ornamenting our authenticity with flourishes of pride, anger, jealousy, possessiveness, and the like. Such a masquerade in fact disguises our inner authenticity as *exaggeration*, in which we seek to make a big deal out of ourselves. Ironically, the more we try to "puff ourselves up," the more we simply exaggerate who we are already. We overdramatize with anger or arrogance in hopes of assuring ourselves that we are who we are. This kind of circular confusion is difficult to unravel because it constantly needs to confirm itself. On the other hand, it is quite simple to stop because it is totally unnecessary. So, establishing our wangthang is easy because such primordial confidence is always with us but difficult because it requires us to stop kidding ourselves and overcome profoundly ingrained self-deceptions.

The key to establishing wangthang, of course, is practicing mindfulness meditation. Such a practice in its sheer simplicity can help us let go of our self-deceptions, synchronize ourselves with our immediate environment, and ultimately inspire others with a deep sense of confidence. But whether we choose to develop our inner authenticity through traditional Buddhist meditation or through other means, wangthang unfolds both gradually and suddenly—gradually, in that our confidence in opening to our world increases over time, and suddenly, in that when we find ourselves open, we are fully open: we cannot be half open; it's all or nothing.

To establish wangthang as mindful leaders is to work on ourselves, but such authentic confidence does not happen in a vacuum. In the final analysis, wangthang is an unfolding from the inside out—a field of power that engages, appreciates, and lends a hand to others—and traditionally, leaders who express such a field of power are said to exhibit four marks: elegance, command, gentleness, and intelligence.

Elegance

A common refrain I have heard from many executives over the years goes something like this: "Look, I'm a straight shooter— I speak my mind honestly and let people know how I see things. I don't play the political game. What you see is what you get." On the surface, such a statement seems worthy. Being a straight shooter, speaking our mind, not playing the political game— all seem quite sincere and, in some sense, authentic. But when we probe beneath the surface, we often find that such statements are merely excuses for being stubborn rather than adapting to what the situation needs.

Leading requires that we work with many different types of people who have many different types of issues and problems. Truck drivers, physicists, college professors, financiers—all require different styles of support, interest, and leadership. The work world is richly diverse, and it is wholly inadequate—at times, even careless—to be simply a "straight shooter" if we expect to lead in such a complex setting. What is required when working with such diversity is elegance.

When we think of elegance, we may picture a cheetah in full stride, a Japanese tea ceremony, or an exquisite Rembrandt. And it is true that such inspiring beauty can be said to be elegant, indeed. In the tradition of the mindful leader, however, elegance is how we express a natural decorum that is fitting to whatever situation we find ourselves in. Because we are fully synchronized, we are never out of step with what is occurring. We move in perfect accord with our circumstances, as if dancing.

Leaders who have established some relationship with this elegance—even in brief, fleeting glimpses—understand how to be comfortable in all settings and are drawn to the uniqueness of what they engage. There is no formula for leading elegantly—no particular theater or one-dimensional style that we bring to the situation. There is no struggle to fit in, so to speak. Rather, mindful leaders who are elegant know how to *be* naturally in the world, adapting to what is presented, listening to what is said, appreciating the distinctive contours of circumstances. Such ease and comfort are basically full of humor because there is no threat, and such leaders do not take themselves seriously but are far more fascinated and delighted with the circumstances that are unfolding. Traditionally, it is said that such elegance "nourishes what needs to be nourished; pacifies what needs to be pacified; destroys what needs to be destroyed."

Such ease with diverse circumstances has a refreshing dignity that is not disturbed by the difficulties of organizational politics. In fact, rather than seeing politics as some kind of distortion or offense, mindful leaders who are elegant experience politics as basically good table manners—an expression of natural decorum. Unlike the straight shooter who is one-dimensional when influencing and communicating, the mindful leader who is elegant serves up ideas with distinction. Just as with serving a meal, political sensibilities require timing, style, and grace, which are natural expressions of wangthang.

During my years in publishing, I worked closely with a senior executive, David, who exhibited outstanding glimmers of wangthang in how he handled himself politically. Well educated, sharply intelligent, and emotionally even, he spent tremendous amounts of time understanding others' needs. Whether on the phone, in meetings, or over dinner, David spent more time listening and learning than any other executive I ever met.

David was often thought of as being inscrutable, for he rarely needed to express his personality, though his style and presence were unmistakable. He never openly vied for attention or power, though it was always accorded to him. He tended to let others speak first; inevitably, his point of view would be expressed by someone else, and he would simply amplify. And before any major decisions were made in the company, confidential calls would be made to seek out his counsel and views. David's political table manners were impeccable, and his skillfulness was elegance in motion.

To be sure, the elegance of wangthang is not mere political slickness or marketing spin. Rather, such elegance is an ease of being, a natural decorum—an enthusiastic willingness to intelligently engage work and life in all their diversity with genuine curiosity and humor.

Command

When we listen to Martin Luther King Jr.'s historic "I Have a Dream" speech, delivered on the steps of the Lincoln Memorial, it is almost impossible not to be moved and inspired. Dr.

King's wangthang is so forceful and compelling that we are exalted on the spot. In fact, no matter how many times we listen to the speech, it seems impossible for it to become routine. We cannot say, "Oh yeah, I heard that speech before. That's that historic dream speech. Real nice." Dr. King's vigor and power in his "I Have a Dream" speech are so undeniable because he expresses wangthang—a command of the situation.

In politics as well as business, commanding the situation is often shorthand for abuse, arrogance, and narcissism. We are all quite familiar with the way that oppressive people at work can often be celebrated as "assertive," "type A," or "go-getters." Take, for example, the case of John Bolton, the former U.S. ambassador to the United Nations, who was widely described by senators, diplomats, and staff as "a serial abuser," "a bully," "a kiss-up, kick-down sort of guy," and by some psychologists as exhibiting many of the symptoms of a psychopath. But, as in many cases in which "command" is misunderstood, such serious shortcomings are sugarcoated with phrases such as "He's a tough-minded diplomat," and "He pursues hard-line policies." For mindful leaders, such arrogance and supposed toughness are the opposite of "commanding the situation" and are in fact the source of much of the toxicity that infects our workplaces and our world in general. Such aggression is sham confidence masquerading as authority, which may produce short-term results but in the long run only serves to create resentment and further confusion.

Traditionally, the command of wangthang is likened to the sun, where a leader's authentic presence is so undeniable and filled with power that others are inescapably nourished and inspired. The sun is not aggressively trying to prove a point or win anyone over. Instead, such command naturally abides and radiates—synchronizing with its surroundings, just as the sun does with the Earth. There is no argument between the sun and the world it nourishes. In fact, the command of the sun adapts perfectly to all needs, providing clarity and enrichment to all creatures large and small. This power of command is not the conventional "top-down" leadership, which is often called the "chain of command." Rather, the command of wangthang is how a mindful leader naturally radiates authenticity from the inside out, inspiring the best in others, just as the sun nourishes all it touches.

I recall a story told to me by a close friend, Kevin, who, as a former navy nurse, traveled around the world offering his medical services to those most in need. His journeys brought him to orphanages in Vietnam, hospitals in Mexico, and hospices in New York City. One of his assignments was with Mother Teresa's nuns in Calcutta. The Indian government had provided Mother with an abandoned military aircraft hangar for housing some of the thousands of homeless dying people whom the nuns rescued from the streets of Calcutta and then bathed and comforted in their final hours. Kevin was assigned as a nurse to this particular hangar. As he told the story, the hangar had become severely overcrowded one day, and the heat was unusually oppressive, intensified by the hangar's metal roof. Despite the heat, swarming flies, and pervasive suffering, Kevin and the nuns worked hard to provide creature comforts, but the situation was desperate, and the many dying patients rioted. Beds were tipped over, medical tables were tossed, angry screaming could be heard, and panic was rising. The head nun instructed another to "run and get Mother," and all the attendants moved to a distance and watched as the riot grew out of control.

Then, suddenly, at the far end of the hangar appeared Mother Teresa, silhouetted by the hot, blazing sunlight outside. And as Kevin told the story, she simply stood there—a small, seemingly frail presence, quiet and barely noticeable as those rioting gradually recognized her. And at such a desperate moment, Kevin recalled vividly that he experienced a deep sense of tenderness—a profound kindness and sadness seemed to pervade the atmosphere, which brought him and dozens of others to tears. In a few moments, the riot slowly calmed, and those who were able began to clean up—righting the beds, helping the seriously ill, and quietly straightening up the hangar. Mother stood for a while longer, saying nothing as everyone worked to bring order. After a few moments, she turned and left.

While I never had the good fortune to meet Mother Teresa, I have long studied her words and consider her one of the great leaders of the twentieth century. And stories such as that of my friend Kevin are apparently not unusual. Whether she was in the presence of prime ministers or prostitutes, wealthy donors or dying children, all spoke of her wangthang—her powerful command that transformed otherwise ordinary situations into penetrating, open, and utterly human moments. Her mere presence radiated a genuine command like the sun that inspired the best in others on the spot.

Gentleness

For mindful leaders, the opposite of gentleness is recklessness, in which we engage life out of panic and create a mess for others. When we are reckless, small irritations such as a stain on our dress can throw us into foolish tantrums or larger problems such as becoming unemployed can make us quick to blame others. At work, recklessness is how we neglect our world by struggling to do more, achieve more, and reassure ourselves more, which often creates further problems.

When we recklessly struggle with life's inevitable difficulties, we act as if we were on an alien planet, feeling threatened and inadequate, as if there were insufficient oxygen or food or water. Even simple activities such as cutting bread or riding a bike become foreign, and we warn one another, "Be careful, don't cut your fingers off with the knife" and "Be careful, wear your helmet, you might fall and crack your head open!" But in fact, we are not being care*ful* at all; we are being care*less* because we *care less* about our actual experience and more about surviving in a seemingly alien world. For mindful leaders, being threatened by bread knives and bicycles is an indication that we are being reckless, unsynchronized, and out of touch with our wangthang.

When we synchronize and open to our experience, we discover that we are not on an alien planet but instead are at home on this Earth, and we can relax, take care, and even enjoy our life. Rather than throwing a tantrum when we stain our dress or lose a business deal, we do what is needed to rectify the problem because it is natural to keep our home in order. Instead of being afraid of cutting our fingers with a knife or making a poor decision when taking a new job, such routine tasks become part of being at home. We understand how to be precise and deliberate in our actions—such things are not foreign. We are not intimidated when we discover a leak in the roof or receive an unexpected bill, complaining bitterly that the world is against us. Instead, we simply deal with the situation. In fact, the gentleness of wangthang reveals that when we fully experience the sense of being at home, we are willing to clean up and repair all kinds of things. We are not afraid to apologize or lend a hand during conflict; we are willing to pick up the cereal box that has accidentally fallen to the grocery store floor or help a colleague refocus a project that has gone awry, because this is our home. Wherever we go, we are not *protecting* our lives but *being* at home, capable of treating the entire situation with the warmth and tenderness that we would extend to our household, family, friends, and neighborhood. As the famed Zen master and political refugee Thich Nhat Hanh observes, "Even if you have the feeling that you don't belong to any land, to any country, to any geographical spot, to any cultural heritage or to any particular ethnic group, you have a true home. . . . Your true home is not an abstract idea. It is something that you can touch and live in every moment."[1]

While the gentleness that arises from being synchronized may make us feel at home, there is also an edge: a penetrating—at times, disturbing—hypersensitivity that is simultaneously both soft yet terrifying. An old woman straightening her dress, a young couple purchasing groceries, or even the color yellow can at times become so poignant in our witnessing that we ache. My teacher, Chögyam Trungpa, likened such exposure to standing atop a Himalayan peak, naked and fully open to the sharp, penetrating chill of the crisp blue sky. There are no guarantees or emotional security deals when it comes to gentleness, just exposure—and remaining in touch with such openness is tremendously demanding, requiring unparalleled courage and commitment.

I once met with a physician who had worked with victims of the 9/11 attack on the World Trade Center. She had spent many hours over many weeks opening to victims and families, counseling grieving loved ones, and caring for the injured. Yet it was clear in our conversation that the doctor had become deeply distressed and a bit distant, concluding that the challenge was too big and awesome, and she felt ill prepared and disappointed in herself. The more she had opened, the larger the tragedy had loomed; the more she lent a helping hand, the more her patients' grief festered. The more she stood atop the mountain fully exposed, the more challenging her world appeared. And she recoiled and stepped back, exhausted.

The doctor's gentle openness was how she directly touched and helped her many patients who were desperately in need of her support and medical attention. Yet such dire circumstances revealed that to gently synchronize with her world was also to feel *unprepared and deeply exposed.* The gentleness of the mindful leader reveals that to be synchronized is to be in tune with a world that demands intimacy first and foremost and offers few, if any, reassurances.

I remember pausing and quietly appreciating this noble woman's hopes and fears, and simply saying, "It's always too early." And right there, together, we both realized that when it comes to actually opening to our world, we never feel prepared, just *exposed.*

Such an understanding is central to establishing our wang-thang as mindful leaders. If we are going to synchronize with our world and be at home, we will have to trust ourselves to lead with our heart without scripts, deals, and preparation. In fact, our gentleness is how we step in over our head and confidently take on life's problems and joys, challenges and passions. As with our doctor, our gentleness is *how we feel when we synchronize*—how we swim in the deep end of life's pool— and such tenderness is precisely the courage and dignity we hope to inspire in others.

Intelligence

When we synchronize and express wangthang, we discover that our senses are in a perpetual dialogue with an intelligent world. Objects such as cups and tree limbs no longer register as flat and two-dimensional but radiate sharp uniqueness and depth. Routine moments no longer pass as uneventful but expose themselves as penetrating exchanges. Tastes, sights, sounds—the full range of sensuality seems to step out from behind a cloud, and our senses glow with clarity, intensely sensitive to the brilliance and vastness of being. As described by my teacher, Chögyam Trungpa:

> Sense perceptions are regarded as sacred. They are regarded as basically good. They are a natural gift, a natural ability that human beings have. They are a source of wisdom. If you don't see sights, if you don't hear sounds, if you don't taste food, you have no way to communicate with the phenomenal world at all. But because of the extraordinary vastness of perception, you have the possibilities of communicating with the depth of the world, the world of sight, the world of sound—the greater world.
>
> In other words, your sense faculties give you access to possibilities of greater perception. Beyond ordinary perception, there is super-sound, super-smell, and super-feeling existing in your being. These can be experienced only by training yourself in the depth of meditation practice, which clarifies any confusion or cloudiness and brings out the precision, sharpness and wisdom of perception—the nowness of your world.[2]

Traditionally, such a vivid interchange between our senses and our world is considered the ultimate wisdom—a sacred intelligence that demands that we acknowledge and fully engage three noble rules: karma, intimacy, and *tendrel.*

Karma We are all familiar with the rule of karma, of course—better known as "cause and effect." Plant a seed and a flower will grow. Run enough stop signs and you will collide with a vehicle crossing your path. Smile at a child often and she will smile back. Cheat your neighbor and you will end up cheating yourself. In the tradition of the mindful leader, respecting this principle of cause and effect is facing the facts of life, which is fundamental if we wish to have a clear, intelligent conversation with reality.

Intimacy Once we develop respect for karma, we then learn that life makes another demand: intimacy. Again, we are all familiar with this principle, which is that each of our lives is utterly personal: love doesn't just hurt, it hurts *personally;* anger isn't just a waste of time, it is *our* waste of time; joy is an exquisite flame, but it can only burn as a unique person. To synchronize and express wangthang is to understand that reality demands intimate exchange, not security or tidiness or accomplishment, and for mindful leaders, dropping our aggression and permitting our hearts to be open and vulnerable is essential if we wish to manifest sacred intelligence.

Tendrel Finally, since we are willing to face the facts of life and admit that our hearts are open, we discover that our world is masterfully intelligent, composing poetry, shaping puns, and playing with humor—crafting endless teachings out of the sensuality that surrounds us:

▶ We have an argument with our lover, storm out of the house in an uproar, and decide to cool off at the local bar over a beer. Moments pass and we begin to overhear a heated conversation between two customers that echoes word for word the very argument we just had, and suddenly we see our blind spot and understand how to apologize.

▶ Otto Loewi, a German-born pharmacologist who won the Nobel Prize in Physiology or Medicine in 1936 for his work on the chemical transmission of nerve impulses, received the design for his initial experiment in a dream.

▶ We're in a meeting with a group of executives trying to figure out how to cut salaries for the company's ten thousand employees, a lunch of fresh sushi is delivered, and one executive, unaware of the delivery, naively observes out loud, "Something stinks in here!"

▶ A Hindu goddess named Namakkal would appear to Srinivasa Ramanujan, a mathematician at Cambridge University, and present mathematical formulas, which he would later refine and verify when applying them to the advancement of such topics as the analytical theory of numbers and infinite series.

These seemingly extraordinary, somewhat humorous, moments are in fact how sacred intelligence unfolds as an utterly synchronized moment—*tendrel,* or interdependent connections. As with the examples above, we are all familiar with such serendipitous moments, but when we synchronize and express wangthang, they are no longer exceptional experiences, and we discover that such playfulness and wisdom are a sacred intelligence woven throughout every moment of the day. Through tendrel, we discover that as much as we seek to lead and inspire, we are also being led and inspired by our world—as if the entire situation were conspiring to make us more healthy, more capable, and more helpful to others. And, as Thich Nhat Hanh suggests here, such understanding of tendrel can be glimpsed in the simplest of moments:

> The next time you have a tangerine to eat, please put it in the palm of your hand and look at it in a way that makes the tangerine real. Your do not need a lot of time to do it, just two to three seconds. Looking at it, you can see a beautiful blossom with sunshine and rain, and you can see a tiny fruit forming. You can see the continuation of the sunshine and the rain and the transformation of the baby fruit into a fully developed tangerine in your hand. You can see the color change from green to orange and you can see the tangerine sweetening. Looking at a tangerine in this way, you will see that everything in the cosmos is in it—sunshine, rain, clouds, trees, leaves, everything. Peeling the tangerine, smelling it, and tasting it, you can be very happy.[3]

PART FOUR
PRACTICES AND EXERCISES

T RAINING EFFECTIVE, inspiring leaders is a pressing priority for all organizations. Businesses compete for capable executives, militaries rigorously shape officers, and the Girl Scouts instill confidence in young women. And whether it's Little League or the corporate boardroom, such training is highly practical because it demands that we become leaders by actually leading. We are put on the spot in circumstances that become our teacher, and we lead to our capacity.

There is no substitute for the rigors of this kind of applied leadership training, and in the tradition of the mindful leader, there are stories of street sweepers, grave diggers, queens, farmers, generals, and even gamblers and beggars who were trained through their livelihoods to become great leaders. Today, however, our modern society offers us the best opportunities in history to train as leaders, whether at work, in colleges, or in government or other institutions. Yet expressing the natural talents of a mindful leader requires something more than being trained in a particular field—as a doctor, a businessperson, a general, or an educator. The training of a mindful leader requires that we commit to *being* first and foremost, and such wisdom is the visceral substance of leadership; it is how we synchronize and open; it is the source of wangthang. Traditionally, we develop this wisdom of being through the disciplines of meditation and contemplation.

18

MEDITATION

MINDFULNESS meditation is the fundamental and indispensable practice of the mindful leader. As we have seen throughout this book, by sitting down and remaining still, we rediscover our natural talents for being patient, open, and humble. And over time, the mindfulness we develop in the practice naturally unfolds on the job —indeed, throughout our entire lives—offering us the opportunity to express the talents of a mindful leader.

Many spiritual traditions teach the value of mindfulness meditation—Zen, Theravada, Confucianism, and Taoism, to name a few. And while the various traditions have much in common, each one offers a unique flavor or nuance in its training that reflects its skill and style. The instructions offered here come from the Kagyu-Nyingma tradition of Tibetan Buddhism and present what is called a Vajrayana form. In this tradition, it is recommended that we receive instruction face-to-face from a person who is trained and authorized to impart such teachings. This way the inevitable questions and concerns can be addressed. In the resources section at the end of the book, I provide information that will help you find an authorized meditation teacher in your area (or visit my website at www.awakeatwork.net).

POSTURE

Begin by sitting upright, relaxed and alert. Keep your eyes open, with a soft gaze that is slightly downward. Hands are placed palms down, gently resting on the thighs. Your chin is tucked in, your face and jaw are relaxed, and your mouth is slightly open. If sitting on the floor, sit on a cushion with your legs loosely crossed. Or you may choose to sit in a chair with your feet firmly on the ground.

In this posture, breathe normally and sit still. Under all circumstances, your posture remains the same: upright, composed, and relaxed.

**THE POSTURE OF MEDITATION, SEATED ON
A MEDITATION CUSHION OR ON A CHAIR.**

THINKING AND LABELING

When we begin to sit, we may notice the simple vividness of our immediate circumstances: the faint sound of passing traffic, the color of our rug, the gentle pressure of our hands on our thighs. For a moment, our senses become sharply alive, and our experience in the present becomes uncomplicated and straightforward.

We will also notice that we are thinking: talking to ourselves, commenting on this and that, ruminating about any number of things. Particularly if we are sitting for the first time, we may find ourselves unusually restless with our thoughts. Such restlessness is not a problem; it is what we work with in sitting.

Attending to these two experiences—being alert in the immediate moment and thinking—is central to sitting practice, and there is a simple instruction for how to work with them properly. When you notice yourself thinking, label it by silently saying to yourself "thinking" and then bring your attention gently back to your out-breath. No matter what the content of your thoughts, simply label them "thinking" and bring your attention back to now by attending to your breath.

One of the challenges of mindfulness meditation is relating skillfully to our thoughts and emotions. They can appear to be like intrusions or nests; enemies or lovers; scorecards or trivia. At times, our thoughts and emotions can slyly convince us that our very existence depends upon keeping them in order and properly cared for. When we practice **mindfulness meditation**, however, we no longer engage our emotions and thoughts as a matter of survival, but instead we touch each one with a gentle ease of respect. We do not have to discard unruly emotions; we do not have to roll our eyes in frustration, fed up with meandering reminiscences. We just touch each thought gently with the label "thinking." Such gentleness is basic to the practice and has tremendous power.

ATTENDING TO THE OUT-BREATH

Maintaining your posture, breathe normally, placing your awareness on the out-breath. Attend to the out-breath gently. The quality of your attention should be "not too loose, not too tight," as my teacher liked to say. We don't get pushy, trying too hard to attend to our breath, and we don't get too lax, spacing out or wandering mentally. Attending to the out-breath requires patience and vigilance, but over time, the mind begins to rest with the out-breath, and you will find that you can keep your attention on your out-breath like gently running your hand over a piece of silk. Slowly, deliberately, again and again, gently place your attention on your out-breath, and eventually you find a natural openness—a balance in which you are synchronized, breathing in the immediate moment.

GENERAL REMARKS

To cultivate an ongoing sitting practice, you'll want to keep to a regular schedule each day. Sessions should be deliberately started and ended, preferably with some signal such as a bell or clap. At first, fifteen minutes in the morning or evening will be ample time, but it will be beneficial to gradually extend your practice, sitting thirty, forty, or perhaps sixty minutes a day. But it's important to begin where you can and not to force yourself. You can extend the duration of your sitting period naturally rather than feeling pushed or obliged. It is recommended that you set aside a special place to meditate, one that is uncluttered and free from distractions. You may choose to buy a meditation cushion and other accessories; sitting on a chair or stool is fine as well.

The instructions given here are deceptively simple, so I encourage you to take your time and work with them gradually and wholeheartedly. Many wonderful books have been written about sitting meditation. There are also some good audio programs available to guide you through a practice session. See the resources section for a list of helpful books and audio programs.

19

CONTEMPLATION

WHEN WE THINK of contemplation, images of cloistered monks and nuns silently moving about the shadows of a monastery may come to mind. This sort of approach to contemplation has its benefits, no doubt. However, for mindful leaders, the original Greek meaning of contemplating offers broader possibilities: to *contemplate* is to "carefully and wisely observe from an open place." Such an open place is familiar territory for mindful leaders, for it is the basic ground of our mind, and from here, by *carefully and wisely observing*, we can gain confidence in leading a dignified and uplifted life.

Contemplation need not be overly complicated. Take, for example, a grasshopper. If we were walking in the park and a grasshopper landed near us, chances are we would stroll right past or maybe give a passing glance of interest. But if we were to "contemplate" the grasshopper—*carefully and wisely observe it from an open place*—we might learn some unexpected lessons. Maybe we would marvel at its ability to fly and imagine how such ability on a human scale would radically change our relationship with our spouse. Or maybe we would consider its color and shape and notice how it powerfully announces itself while perfectly blending into its surroundings at the same time—a wonderful political trick, indeed. Or maybe by wisely observing a grasshopper, we would glimpse how profound and playful infinite space can be, expressing itself as a chirping, leaping, careening bug.

Contemplation, in its most basic form, is our ability to appreciate our world, which tenderizes us—marinating our toughness, dissolving our resistance, and opening us further to the marvels, suffering, and intimacy of life. Such appreciation actually protects us as mindful leaders, for it keeps us vigilant and synchronized.

SIX-STEP CONTEMPLATION

There are many traditions of contemplation, but all forms essentially seek to make spiritual insight immediate, personal, and real—more than just an accumulation of lessons taught by other people. To contemplate is to discover directly the truth of the matter—to unmistakably understand and appreciate the circumstances in which we find ourselves.

As with sitting meditation, it is always best to get instruction from teachers who are well trained in such contemplative disciplines. For the most part, my training in contemplation comes from the Tibetan Buddhist tradition of analytical *vipassyana* and *tonglen*. Essentially, these practices guide us in carefully considering the natural passing of events and in generating loving-kindness toward others. The six-step contemplation suggested below is inspired by my training in these practices as well as some experience with the Confucian practice of *Chuching,* or "abiding in reverence." While I have not had the opportunity to train directly with a master of Chu-ching, I have relied extensively on an excellent work on this practice by Rodney Taylor, PhD, *The Confucian Way of Contemplation,* which explores the teachings of Okada Takehiko, one of the great Confucian teachers of the twentieth century.

The process of contemplation I recommend is as follows:

1. Rest the mind in the present moment.
2. Shift to contemplation.
3. Actively consider the object.
4. Permit insight to touch the heart.
5. Conclude with an aspiration.
6. Disown the experience.

1. Rest the Mind in the Present Moment

All contemplations of the mindful leader begin with a moment of mindfulness meditation in which we simply rest in the present moment, synchronized and attuned with our circumstances. Typically, this first short gesture of mindfulness can last two to ten minutes, depending on circumstances, and need not be conducted while sitting on a meditation cushion. When preparing for contemplation, we can more actively pacify discursiveness by gently acknowledging our thoughts as worthy of our attention, but not at this moment. When a thought arises, we may say to ourselves, "This is an important thought, but let me set it aside for now and attend to it later." By carefully acknowledging thoughts, placing them on hold, and then coming back to our immediate circumstances, we create the ground for contemplating—settled, still, and synchronized.

2. Shift to Contemplation

Once we are resting in the present moment, we shift to contemplative activity, but such activity is different from achievement-oriented behavior. Just as with mindfulness meditation, we contemplate with no intention of cultivating a particular state of mind. We consider the object of contemplation—whether it be a reading, physical object, or mental reflection—from the place of openness. We soak in the object of contemplation—fully appreciating whatever it offers. Our contemplative activity becomes an expression of synchronized mind rather than an attempt to learn a lesson. Consequently, when we shift to contemplative activity, we gently preserve the mind of nonachievement—settled, still and synchronized. As Kusumoto Tanzan, the great nineteenth-century Confucian scholar, suggests, we contemplate from a naked yet profound perspective:

> At the point when one calms the mind by quiet sitting, the eyes see color as it actually is, the ears hear sound as it actually is, the nose smells odor as it actually is, the movement of the hands and feet is in accord with the process of creation of things as they actually are; the substance of the mind becomes vigorous. . . . It is unfathomable and still like a deep abyss, it is broad and expansive like heaven. Everything becomes whole and one and merges together.[1]

3. Actively Consider the Object

When contemplating, the object we consider can be a reading, an issue or a problem, a spiritual instruction, a physical object, an activity, or a visualized image. Whatever we choose to contemplate, our task is to *carefully and wisely appreciate* what is unfolding. Unlike conventional learning—in which we may tend to analyze, deconstruct, dispute, and generally seek to conceptually grasp the matter at hand—in contemplation, we are vigorously opening to the object, permitting our natural intelligence, curiosity, and warmth to *know directly* the matter at hand. Such opening will require that we sharply engage our experience—synchronized, still, and settled. And, just as with sitting meditation, we may have a tendency to distract ourselves from our experience, but we do not treat such discursiveness as an enemy. Rather than coming back to our breath when we are distracted, in contemplation, we return our attention to our activity. For example, in the *mindful eating* contemplation (presented in the next chapter), we will surely become distracted at some point, but we return by directing our attention back to eating our meal. We need not label a thought or attend to our breath; we simply notice our distraction and open once again to our contemplative activity. When we shift back, we may notice that we are once again fully synchronized, carefully and wisely appreciating our experience.

4. Permit Insight to Touch the Heart

As we contemplate, we may notice that we personally and intimately understand. Such insight can be exhilarating, like letting go of a huge weight, or it can be heartbreaking, like having no skin and permitting life's sadness to strike us to the core. Other times such knowing can be like the wind—free and easy and delightful. The range of wisdom arising out of contemplation is wide and deep, but always—*always*—it touches our most intimate core. Contemplation introduces the possibility of knowing something directly, which requires not only discipline and precision but bravery, because it demands that we permit our hearts to be touched—at times, even ransacked—by reality. The contemplations of the mindful leader may bring us to tears or suggest vast possibilities. Maybe we will have insights that transform our life or simply help us do our job better. In all cases, the insights arising from contemplation gradually dissolve our preconceptions and strengthen our willingness to remain synchronized and directly in touch with our lives.

5. Conclude with an Aspiration

Ending our contemplation requires that we gently lay down the object of contemplation and return our attention to our routine circumstances. When we make this shift, we will notice that while we are no longer contemplating, there remains a lingering sense—a bodily wisdom. Our joy or sadness persists in our chest; our vigor or excitement seems to float on the surface of our skin. Remaining mindful of these sensations without grasping is how we gradually shift and attend to our lives. Traditionally, it is at this point that practitioners end a session of contemplation by making an aspiration. For example, we may choose to end a session with:

> May everyone, everywhere delight in their lives;
> And may they understand the source of such delight.
> May everyone, everywhere be free from fear and
> resentment;
> And may they understand the pointlessness of such
> panic.
> May everyone, everywhere be impartial in extending
> their wisdom and kindness toward the world.

6. Disown the Experience

While we will want to sustain the wisdom and realization we gain from contemplating, *trying* to do so only makes such a possibility that much more unlikely. Consequently, ending contemplation skillfully requires us to refrain from trying to capture the insight that unfolded. This is not to say that we cannot reflect on our experience or even jot down some thoughts that we feel are particularly poignant or helpful. Rather, to disown our experience is to permit our insight to fully shape our being instead of trying to monumentalize it as a thoughtful lesson. Permitting our learning to permeate our being rather than add to our conceptual knowledge is what distinguishes contemplation from conventional learning. It is important, then, to disown our contemplative experience, letting go of any reflection, attending to the present moment, and permitting the lessons learned to organically mix with our heart and mind.

CONTEMPLATIVE STUDY

There is an infinite number of objects for contemplation: nature, music, mental images, bodily sensations, a child's smile. Traditional contemplations, several of which are offered below, often invite us to study and reflect on poems, texts, and instructions. The contemplative study of such material requires that we remain alert to the synchronized aspect of contemplating and not overly intellectualize the practice. As Chu Hsi, the twelfth-century founder of the Cheng-Chu school of neo-Confucianism, explains:

In reading, first collect together mind and body, and quiet the mind a little. Then open a book and it will be far more effective. If the mind is driven toward external things and is chaotic, then the mind is completely separated from the way. In this kind of situation one cannot read. There is no need of any explanation, just simply shut the gate and for a period of ten days to two weeks sit correctly. After that when one looks at books one will understand what I say is not nonsense.[2]

Chu Hsi's instruction is essentially to practice mindfulness "a little" before study and then comprehend the reading in a "more effective" way from a quiet place rather than permit the mind to be chaotically "driven toward external things." He brashly suggests that if we cannot do such a thing, we should go on retreat for two weeks and then resume our studies correctly—an instruction we may want to follow if we have the time and commitment.

Contemplative study can be applied equally to spiritual texts or conventional readings, and in some of my seminars, I have used this technique with participants for reading current scientific material and essays on business. Although I have used this contemplation personally for studying strategic plans and book manuscripts, I have not found it very useful in studying financial plans—nothing seems to lighten such an onerous load.

During contemplative study, use the suggested six-step contemplation and keep the following in mind:

▶ Whenever the mind wanders, bring it back to reading the text and do not struggle to recollect or retrace your steps.

Permit the mind to open and peruse the text lightly like the wind.

▶ On occasion, you may be inclined to record an insight that arises; keep the notes brief and spontaneous. Avoid making extended observations that distract you from reading the text mindfully.

▶ Reading may incline you toward making a decision. You may realize when reading "The Thirty Reminders" (in the following section) that you suddenly understand how to manage a pressing problem or when reading a business plan that the author had bet too much on the success of an emerging technology. Permit such insights to arise but postpone coming to a firm or final decision. Instead, remain open and curious—mindful of the insight but not fixed in its conclusion.

▶ Permit yourself to be influenced by the voice of the author, not just the words; note your emotional and physical reactions and permit them to guide insight without resistance.

▶ Enjoy the sheer pleasure of reading; as if you were sipping fine wine or listening to sublime music, savor the unfolding flavors and appreciate the notes of the literary melody.

In the next section, I offer some adapted traditional teachings for contemplative study: the thirty reminders of the mindful leader and the four reflections of the mindful leader. There is a rich body of material for further contemplative study for those interested. I recommend starting with *The Way of the Bodhisattva* by Shantideva and Pema Chödrön's commentary on it, *No Time to Lose.*

THE THIRTY REMINDERS OF THE MINDFUL LEADER

The thirty reminders below are inspired by the teachings of the Tibetan master Gyalsay Togme Sangpo (1295–1369). Using the six-step contemplation, read all thirty reminders slowly and in order, reflecting on how to live the uplifted life of a mindful leader.

1. Take time to meditate, reflect, and study.
2. Cultivate a household that appreciates the training of a mindful leader.
3. Create moments of silence; retreat to be alone on occasion.
4. Contemplate the impermanent nature of wealth and career.
5. Show respect to those who teach you how to become a mindful leader.
6. On occasion, meditate and study with others who aspire to become mindful leaders.
7. Work hard to open to life's circumstances; step beyond resistance.
8. Permit life to reveal its fundamental nature: free, vast, and confident.
9. Put others ahead of yourself; focus on promoting their welfare.
10. Carefully examine all insults; quietly wish the best to those who are rude.
11. Clean up messes and difficulties, even if they are not of your making.
12. Treat adverse circumstances as your teacher.

13. When hurt by those you trust and love, show kindness.
14. Never lose courage in the face of physical pain and difficult circumstances.
15. When praised, carefully examine your tendency toward pride and arrogance.
16. Take full responsibility for your anger; lay it down gently but quickly.
17. Abandon addiction and compulsive attractions; savor pleasures with dignity.
18. Dispel the blinding effects of making "me" the center of everything.
19. When grieving, contemplate the passing nature of everything.
20. Enjoy bestowing gifts on others.
21. Cultivate your natural tendency to be decent toward others.
22. Patiently invite all that arises—good, bad, happy, sad.
23. Never give up inspiring others and contributing to the world.
24. Rest in the ease of synchronized mind.
25. Recognize that the world is free of your story lines; notice the situation directly.
26. Reflect on your mistakes; make them friends, not enemies.
27. Create a household environment that is uplifted and wise.
28. Abandon harsh language.
29. Be sharp and quick to cut the root of arrogance and stupidity.
30. Dedicate all success to the benefit of others.

THE FOUR REFLECTIONS OF THE MINDFUL LEADER

We can often find ourselves believing our own story line, buying into some fixed version of ourselves. We may conclude that we are successful because we have been awarded a trophy engraved with our name, or maybe we consider ourselves uninspiring because we have recently been divorced, we are currently unemployed, and everything seems to say we are a loser. When we buy into story lines, whatever their content, we lose perspective and make it difficult to lead a dignified life. For mindful leaders, such fixed views of ourselves, whether exciting or depressing, are just self-deception, and in order to preserve a perspective that is synchronized with the circumstances in which we find ourselves, mindful leaders traditionally contemplate four conditions for being human:

1. The human body is marvelous, fragile, and difficult to come by.
2. Everything changes, and death is inevitable.
3. All actions have a result.
4. There is tremendous suffering in the world.

These four conditions of life have been contemplated by millions of people for thousands of years, and they form the basis for how a mindful leader remains in touch with the simple realities of being human.

Contemplate "The human body is marvelous, fragile, and difficult to come by"
Using the six-step contemplation, read the instructions below, pausing after each one to carefully reflect.

1. Observe your toes and fingers, hair follicles and nostrils. Inside organs and outside skin. Scan your body slowly from head to toe.
2. Can you find "you"?
3. Appreciate the marvels of being a body in space: flex your fingers, turn your head from left to right, and take a breath or two.
4. Consider that one out of five Americans is physically disabled. Reflect on what it would be like to lose power over your arms or legs. Close your eyes and reflect on the possibility of becoming blind.
5. Carefully consider the conditions required for a human body to appear. For example, if the Earth's angle of inclination to the sun were to shift a mere ten degrees, conditions would become too hot or too cold to sustain human life.
6. Consider this old Tibetan tale: If there were only one turtle in the world swimming in an ocean that covered the entire planet, and as its head broke the surface of the water for the very first time, you happened to be throwing a life preserver randomly upon the surface of that very same ocean, and coincidentally the turtle's head appeared inside the ring of the tossed life preserver as it struck the water, the likelihood that such a coincidence could happen is equal to the likelihood that human birth could appear in infinite space.
7. Consider this Tibetan poem:

> This free and favorable life, very difficult to obtain,
> Brings the accomplishment of the purpose of
> human existence.

I will appreciate this good fortune
And take the opportunity to live a noble life.[3]

Contemplate "Everything changes, and death is inevitable"

Using the six-step contemplation, read the instructions below, pausing after each one to carefully reflect.

1. Inspect your surroundings and notice that nothing is the same. No matter what you consider—trees, cats, taxis, wind patterns, neighbors—nothing is the same. Inspect a leaf closely and see that even a single leaf is not exactly the same moment to moment. Consider carefully the simple fact that nothing is the same.

2. Death can come at any moment, and we all know it. More than 200,000 Americans die every month,[4] and a teenager dies in a car accident in the United States about every ninety minutes.[5] Approximately 16,000 children starve to death every day.[6]

3. Reflect on the millions upon millions of people who have come before you and died. Can anyone remember their names and how they lived their lives? Where are all their possessions today? Consider that each person who has died felt his or her life as intimately and as fully as you feel yours right now. Reflect carefully and wisely on the fact that you will be dead soon.

4. Consider this Tibetan poem:

This world is impermanent like the clouds of autumn.
The birth and death of beings are like a drama you
are watching.

The life of beings passes like a flash of lightning in
the sky.
It goes quickly, like water tumbling down a steep
mountain.[7]

Contemplate "All actions have a result"

Using the six-step contemplation, read the instructions below,
pausing after each one to carefully reflect.

1. Notice that everything leads to something else. A seed
   produces a plant; a breeze produces movement; the sun
   produces warmth on the skin. All actions have a result.
2. Consider carefully how every action you take has a result.
   A smile produces what? Anger produces what? Speed and
   hard work produce what? Reflect on all the actions you
   take throughout the day and what they lead to. Describe
   to yourself what you have created in this world.
3. Reflect on what actions make you feel healthy and resolve
   to do more of those things. Reflect on what actions make
   you feel unhealthy and ponder ways to stop. Consider
   ways that you help others and ways that others help you.
4. If you were about to die, what one piece of advice would
   you have for all other human beings?
5. Consider this Tibetan poem:

   When their time comes, even kings and queens pass
   away,
   And enjoyments, loved ones, and friends cannot
   follow after.
   But wherever beings are, wherever they go,
   The results of their behavior follow after them like
   a shadow.[8]

Contemplate "There is tremendous suffering in the world"

Using the six-step contemplation, read the instructions below, pausing after each one to carefully reflect.

1. Consider that millions of families live homeless, hundreds of thousands die of starvation each week, and war ravages countless lives. Carefully consider your good fortune in having favorable conditions that enable you to make a living or be part of a family. Even if your conditions are challenging and difficult, reflect on the suffering of others and appreciate the ever present quality of human distress.

2. The scope and magnitude of human suffering are both vast and intimate at the same time. While we can contemplate others' suffering, we *experience* suffering one person at a time. Who do you know who is lonely? Who do you know who is angry and bitter? Who do you know who has lost a loved one or become addicted to drugs?

3. Imagine in your mind's eye a small child who has lost her parents and is alone and starving with no one to care for her. Reflect on the fact that thousands of children in the world face this predicament right now.

4. Consider this Tibetan poem:

> Through the power of greed, anger and stupidity,
> We human beings circle helplessly in confusion
> Behaving like arrogant gods, angry demons and ignorant beasts.
> It is like being caught on a spinning potter's wheel.
> The world blazes with this suffering, fearing old age
> and sickness.

There is no protection here from the fiercely blazing
fires of death.
We human beings arise in this world so very confused
And are like bees trapped in a vase, circling.[9]

20

CONTEMPLATIVE ACTIVITY

A PPLYING the six-step contemplation to daily activities can transform our most ordinary experiences into profoundly defining moments, and in the tradition of the mindful leader, thousands of stories have been passed down illustrating how such transformation takes place. For example, consider this traditional Zen story about two monks cleaning the dishes and assisting a cranky bug:

> Two monks were washing their bowls in the river when they noticed a scorpion drowning. One monk scooped it up and set it upon a rock and was stung. He went back to washing his bowl, and again the scorpion fell into the water. The monk scooped the scorpion up and was again stung.
>
> The other monk asked him, "Friend, why do you continue to save the scorpion when you know its nature is to sting?"
>
> "Because," the monk replied, "to save it is my nature."

In contemplative activity—whether we are walking, eating, listening, or saving angry bugs from drowning—we engage ordinary *activities* with the stillness of a synchronized mind and, by doing so, learn profound lessons. Such activity requires that we discover "stillness within the action"—maintaining a state of mind that is settled even in activity. As Ch'eng Hao, an eleventh-century Confucian master, suggests:

> A calm and settled nature is a mind that is calmed and settled whether in a state of quietude or in a state of activity. . . . If you think in terms of internal and external as two separate parts, then the calm and settled nature is something that cannot be obtained.[1]

During the contemplative activities suggested in the following sections, use the six steps for contemplation and keep these guidelines in mind:

▶ Enjoy the expansive quality of the contemplation but remain alert at the same time. When the mind wanders, do not struggle to regain composure but simply bring the mind back to the activity at hand. Permit the mind to open to whatever occurs.

▶ On occasion, you may be inclined to savor an insight or linger over a particularly touching moment, which is fine. Avoid extended reflection, however, which may distract you from spontaneously engaging the moment.

▶ Permit the unique wisdom of the experience to influence you, being careful not to get too caught up in the exercise. In a very real sense, we are not "contemplating" at all but simply appreciating life on its terms.

▶ Be especially aware of your emotional and physical reactions and permit them to guide insight without resistance.

▶ Enjoy the sheer pleasure of walking, eating, and listening and notice on occasion that the melody of circumstance is your most profound teacher.

PRESENCE OF MIND

While the object of this contemplation is a bit subtle, it nonetheless addresses a pervasive feature of how we conduct ourselves throughout the day. As we familiarize ourselves with mindfulness meditation, we become increasingly aware of how we lose touch with our experience. We space out, forget to listen, mull over our worries, and generally find ourselves absentminded rather than mindfully present. This contemplation is to be practiced throughout the entire day, heightening our awareness of the contrast between being present and being out of touch with our lives.

1. Complete steps 1 and 2 of the six-step contemplation, preferably in the morning before you begin your day.
2. During routine activities, notice how and when you become "present." Try to observe the contrast between "presence of mind" and "absentmindedness." How does this shift happen?
3. Notice that being vividly alert and present arises suddenly. Are there any particular events or experiences that invite you to be present? Notice the "haunting" quality of the presence of mind.
4. Carefully observe when you daydream. Do you mull over future possibilities or past occurrences? Are there any circumstances that trigger fears, anxieties, distractions, idle entertainments? How long do daydreams last, and how do they end?

5. Take time to deliberately bring your alertness to the tasks at hand. If you are sitting quietly, notice your surroundings. If you are moving about, carefully observe ordinary, mundane actions: putting on a shoe, brushing your teeth, starting your car.

6. When you notice that you have been distracted for some amount of time, what do you do? What do you think? What do you think you missed? What are you experiencing at the very moment when you reflect on having spaced out?

7. Try to identify what alerts you to being distracted; how is it that you bring you attention back to now?

EATING MINDFULLY

In our fast-paced society, we too often numb our senses, speeding past the smells, sights, and sounds of the world around us. The odor of rain, the vivid blue of the sky, or the rumble of a passing truck are so easily assumed to be uneventful that we miss the enlivening immediacy of being synchronized with such moments. This contemplation of eating mindfully invites us to experience the world through our senses without preconceptions—without judging, assuming, analyzing, or even naming. Using our meals as an object for contemplation offers the opportunity to deliberately slow down and fully drink in our sensual surroundings. Although this contemplation can be done while dining at home, the instructions are to dine out at a restaurant, cultivating a clear and present mind throughout the entire ritual—fully synchronizing with our sensual experience.

1. Complete steps 1 and 2 of the six-step contemplation, mindfully synchronizing, becoming open and settled in the present moment.

2. As you enter the restaurant and prepare to be seated, take careful note of the ambience and atmosphere. Observe the lighting and decor—flowers, paintings, wall color. Notice those who are sharing the entire space with you: other diners, waiters, and waitresses.

3. Once you take your place, observe closely, appreciating how the table is appointed: tablecloth, forks, spoons, plates, and glasses. Consider how you physically feel: cramped, expansive, cozy.

4. Pay careful attention to the quality of service. Is the waiter or hostess rushed, attentive, at ease, gracious? If there are mistakes, oversights, or inadequacies in the service or meal, note them gently but do not amplify them. Be deliberate, courteous, and spacious in responses and questions and take note of the changes in atmosphere. Glance around and observe how others are appreciating their food and dining experience.

5. As courses of the meal are served, attend mindfully and openly to all the senses. Taste the wine and beverages but also appreciate their aroma and color. Taste the food but appreciate how it is "plated" as well. Permit all the senses to synchronize in appreciation.

6. Handle utensils deliberately, appreciating the weight of the fork and knife, the contours of the glass, and the shapes of the plate and bowl. Bring food and drink mindfully *toward* you rather than leaning into the meal.

7. When you find yourself distracted, deliberately come back to the physical setting, lingering over the smells,

tastes, and visual experience. Take note when the mind, body, and atmosphere synchronize as a singular dining moment.

8. Complete this contemplation with steps 5 and 6 of the six-step contemplation: Think of all those in the world in need of a meal and resolve to consider them in the future. Consider also the hard work and discernment the restaurant staff put into serving you a meal.

MINDFULLY ATTENDING MEETINGS

We take part in so many meetings at work, but do we really "attend"? Do we actually listen to one another when we show up, or do we spend most of our time talking to ourselves? While seven out of ten business leaders rank listening as an "extremely important" workplace skill,[2] studies show that we spend 75 percent of our time *not* listening—distracted, preoccupied, or forgetful.[3] And when we do listen, we can recall only 25 to 50 percent of what is said,[4] even when we try to pay attention.

But when we do listen, what are we actually listening to? We seem to spend a lot of time trying to understand one another's words, which is not surprising in a workplace that has become so "word heavy" with e-mails, text messages, and PowerPoint presentations. Mehrabian's rule—named after the distinguished psychologist and engineer Dr. Albert Mehrabian, whose research pioneered the study of nonverbal communications—has shown, however, that only 7 percent of our message is actually communicated through words, while 55 percent is communicated by our body and 38 percent by our tone of voice.[5] That means that over 90 percent of human communication is expressed and understood without words, and the challenge is, can we truly listen to one another? Especially at meetings, can we bring our complete attention to the situation and listen fully?

1. Before attending a meeting, spend a few moments completing steps 1 and 2 of the six-step contemplation. At first, it is best to use this contemplation during meetings in which you are not responsible for running the meeting or making the central contribution.

2. As you enter the meeting, take note of the surroundings. Is the room neatly arranged, untidy, barren? Carefully sense the environment—hurried, somber, cheerful?

3. As you take your seat, mindfully notice the others in the room, appreciating their attire, greeting them deliberately, and observing their behaviors.

4. During the meeting, carefully observe how often you are *thinking about* what others are saying rather than actually *listening to* what is being said. What prevents you from being mindful and present in a conversation? When you notice that you are distracted by your inner commentary, shift your attention back to the present moment. Listen fully to the words, body language, and tone.

5. Notice any tendency you have to make judgments, to agree or disagree, or to overly interpret what another is saying. Set such tendencies aside and listen carefully with no preconceptions.

6. Notice the speed with which the mind jumps to conclusions or exhibits tendencies to "make a point" rather

than fully understand. Which is more interesting: understanding what the other person is trying to communicate or making your point?

7. Be especially attentive to your physical gestures and those of other participants. How are your colleagues positioned? Glance around the room and take note of what each person is communicating nonverbally by posture or by how he or she walks.

8. What unique gestures do others seem to make regularly? How do those gestures make you feel?

9. Carefully observe when a person's words say one thing and the tone of voice conveys something completely different. Which of these messages seems to have a greater impact on you?

10. When appropriate, ask questions and probe to better understand and clarify what others are saying rather than trying to make a point.

AIMLESSLY WANDERING

This contemplation is deceptively simple, for it requires that we just wander without purpose or direction in any setting of our choice. It has the potential, however, to be profoundly revealing. Meandering on beaches, in the woods, down city streets, or even in our backyard provides ample opportunity to engage this contemplation. Be duly warned, however: wandering in unknown territory will inevitably present surprises.

1. Prepare by choosing a general location for your aimless wandering. Establish no goals, destinations, or agendas. Be free of intention.

2. As always, begin the contemplation with steps 1 and 2 of the six-step contemplation.

3. As you begin the contemplation, open out fully: there is nowhere to go and nothing to do.

4. Let go of the need to keep track of anything whatsoever. As the mind seeks to set a course or recollect, drop the internal tracking and bring your attention to whatever is occurring.

5. Permit yourself to appreciate whatever arises. Pause and carefully observe anything that attracts your attention. Give your curiosity free rein with sights, sounds, smells, and physical feelings that spontaneously guide your wandering.

6. Be responsive to environmental cues: a bird bathing in a puddle, designers rearranging a department store window display, the sound of a violin—all are permitted to capture and lead your attention.

7. Acknowledge physical feelings that occur throughout the exercise without unduly lingering with the sensation.

8. Explore surprises and seeming coincidences. Notice and appreciate any excitement that may arise but refrain from embellishing it.

9. Make no deliberate mental notes but simply disown experience as it arises. Quickly drop the tendency to overdramatize contemplative insight.

10. Open physically to the absolute freedom of having nothing to gain and nothing to lose. Marveling at the sheer magnificence of it all is highly recommended.

21

TRAINING THE MIND

A COMMON contemplative practice throughout Tibet is *lojong,* or mind training, drawn from an ancient Buddhist teaching called "The Root Text of the Seven Points of Training the Mind." This contemplative practice involves memorizing and studying fifty-nine pithy slogans, which are shorthand instructions for unraveling self-deception, cultivating compassion, and enlivening wakefulness in everyday life. The slogan practice has been widely used throughout Tibet for more than a thousand years, and many of the great Tibetan spiritual teachers commented on the text, expanding and refining the practice.

Lojong practitioners memorize the fifty-nine slogans so they can easily recall them throughout the day and spontaneously engage in contemplative activity. By staying alert to the slogans in this way, lojong practitioners permit daily events to evoke the slogans' wisdom, revealing ordinary experiences as opportunities to wake up. Daily experience thus becomes contemplation and ordinary life, a spiritual path.

For example, the slogan "Be grateful to everyone" reminds us that we can offer a lot of space to friends and rivals alike. Normally we are quite willing to say thank you to those who help us or give us praise. But the teaching suggests that such a narrow view unnecessarily confines us, limiting our ability to be skillful and open. Instead, "Be grateful to everyone" suggests that we can allow ourselves the freedom to appreciate everyone's concerns, styles, foibles, and talents, and in turn be grateful for what we discover. Such open gratitude appreciates that our friends and adversaries, our competitors and supporters, strangers and friends alike, all teach us valuable lessons and, by being grateful to everyone rather than just those we like or prefer, we discover that we can accommodate just about anything at work with confidence and poise.

One particularly insightful lojong slogan for leaders is "Drive all blames into one." This teaching reminds us to disarm the cowardly and pointless ritual of avoiding responsibility and blaming others. Too often accountability is misused in organizations as a weapon to defeat, humiliate, or marginalize others. Gossip, stubbornness, and aggression of all kinds flow from our need to "blame" others for mistakes, political blunders, or just a slip of the tongue. This slogan instructs us to eliminate such confusion by modeling the freshness of honest accountability and reestablishing candor and openness among others. It urges us to create a new habit in our daily lives: rather than reflexively pointing our fingers at others, we learn to take responsibility.

Mastering the lojong contemplative discipline requires training from an empowered teacher, but there are many excellent commentaries for those interested. To learn more about lojong practice, I recommend:

The Great Path of Awakening: The Classic Guide to Lojong by Jamgon Kongtrul (Shambhala, 2005)

Training the Mind and Cultivating Loving-Kindness by Chögyam Trungpa (Shambhala, 1993)

Enlightened Courage by Dilgo Khyentse (Snow Lion, 1993)

The Practice of Lojong by Traleg Kyabgon (Shambhala, 2007)

Start Where You Are: A Guide to Compassionate Living by Pema Chödrön (Shambhala, 1994)

For guidance on applying the lojong teachings in the context of the workplace, see my previous book, *Awake at Work: 35 Practical Buddhist Principles for Discovering Clarity and Balance in the Midst of Work's Chaos.*

INTRODUCTION

1. These statistics come from the Bread for the World Research Institute, the U.N. Commission on Human Rights, the Natural Resources Defense Council, and the World Health Organization, respectively.

1. OPENING UP TO WORKPLACE REALITIES

1. *Yankelovich Monitor,* March 10, 2003.
2. *Journal of Psychosomatic Research,* 1997.
3. American Institute of Stress.
4. Bruce Chadwick, Ph.D., "George Washington's War," *Sourcebook,* 2005.

2. OVERCOMING SELF-DECEPTION

1. Chögyam Trungpa Rinpoche, *Training the Mind* (Boston: Shambhala, 2005), 70–71.

3. THE ART OF SITTING STILL

1. Sharon Begley, *Train Your Mind, Change Your Brain* (New York: Random House, 2007); Jon Kabat-Zinn, *Coming to Our Senses* (New York: Hyperion, 2005).
2. Shunryu Suzuki, *Zen Mind, Beginner's Mind* (Boston: Shambhala, 2006).

4. SIMPLICITY

1. Richard Saul Wurman, *Information Anxiety* (New York: Doubleday, 1989), 33.
2. "Overloaded Circuits: Why Smart People Underperform," *Harvard Business Review,* January 2005.

5. POISE

1. Forum hosted by *Harvard Negotiation Law Review*, Harvard University, Cambridge, Mass., March 8, 2002. ADR stands for "alternative dispute resolution."

7. COURAGE

1. Kathleen D. Ryan and Daniel K. Oestreich, *Driving Fear Out of the Workplace* (San Francisco: Jossey-Bass, 1991).
2. Harvey A. Hornstein, *Managerial Courage* (Hoboken, N.J.: Wiley, 1986).

9. ENTHUSIASM

1. Chögyam Trungpa, *Shambhala: The Sacred Path of the Warrior* (Boston: Shambhala, 1997), 63.

10. PATIENCE

1. From a study conducted by the Royal Sun Alliance for National Stress Awareness Day in Britain, 2006.
2. Translated from the Pali by Thanissaro Bhikkhu, the abbot of Metta Forest Monastery, San Diego, California.
3. Chögyam Trungpa Rinpoche, *The Myth of Freedom* (Boston: Shambhala, 2005), 71.

11. AWARENESS

1. Daniel Goleman, "What Makes a Leader?", *Harvard Business Review*, 1998.

13. HUMILITY

1. Bernie Glassman, "Bearing Witness," *Bell Tower* 1998.

16. INSPIRING HEALTH AND WELL-BEING IN ORGANIZATIONS

1. Peter J. Frost, *Toxic Emotions at Work* (Cambridge, Mass.: Harvard Business School, 2003), 85.
2. Ibid., 190.

3. Donald Rumsfeld, U.S. secretary of defense, speaking at a press conference in 2002.

4. Frost, 180.

17. ESTABLISHING AUTHENTICITY

1. Thich Nhat Hanh, "Returning Home," *Shambhala Sun*, March 2006, 62.

2. *The Collected Works of Chögyam Trungpa*, vol. 8 (Boston: Shambhala, 2004), 81.

3. Thich Nhat Hanh, "The Art of Living," in Claude Whitmyer, ed., *Mindfulness and Meaningful Work* (Berkeley, Calif.: Parallax Press, 1994).

19. CONTEMPLATION

1. Rodney L. Taylor, *The Confucian Way of Contemplation* (University of South Carolina Press, 1988), 51.

2. Ibid., 38.

3. Adapted from *The Blissful Path to Liberation: The Liturgy for the Preliminaries Drawn from The Ornament of the Mind of Guru Padmakara, the Practice Manual for The Very Profound Sacred Great Perfection Sadhana of the Embodiment of the Three Jewels* (Könchok Chidü ngöndro) by Jamgön Kongtrül the Great.

4. *National Vital Statistics Report* 53, no. 15.

5. The *National Highway Traffic Safety Administration Research Note*, March 2006, reports 7,570 fatalities for ages eight to twenty in 2003.

6. Bread for the World Research Institute.

7. Adapted from *The Blissful Path to Liberation*.

8. Ibid.

9. Ibid.

20. CONTEMPLATIVE ACTIVITY

1. Taylor, 80.

2. Michael Purdy, "The Listener Wins," article posted on www.monster.com.

3. Rosemary Horton, "On Listening," Trinity College of Western Australia, P. L. Duffy Resource Center.

4. Dick Lee and Delmar Hatesohl, "Listening: Our Most Used Communication Skill," University of Missouri, 1993.

5. Albert Mehrabian, *Silent Messages* (Belmont, Calif.: Wadsworth, 1971).

.

RESOURCES

THE PRACTICE OF MEDITATION

Books

Chödrön, Pema. *The Wisdom of No Escape and the Path of Loving-Kindness.* Boston: Shambhala, 2001.

Lee, Cyndi. *Yoga Body, Buddha Mind.* New York: Riverhead Trade, 2004.

Suzuki, Shunryu. *Zen Mind, Beginner's Mind.* Boston: Weatherhill, 1986.

Taylor, Rodney L., PhD. *The Confucian Way of Contemplation.* Columbia: University of South Carolina Press, 1988.

Trungpa, Chögyam. *The Path Is the Goal: A Basic Handbook of Buddhist Meditation.* Boston: Shambhala, 1995.

Audio Programs

Loori, John Daido. *Finding the Still Point: A Beginner's Guide to Zen Meditation.* Book and CD. Boston: Shambhala, 2007.

Piver, Susan. *Joyful Mind: A Practical Guide to Buddhist Meditation.* Book and CD. New York: Rodale, 2002.

Practice Centers and Organizations

The Garrison Institute
Garrison, N.Y.
845-424-4800
www.garrisoninstitute.org/home.php

Insight Meditation Society
1230 Pleasant Street
Barre, MA 01005
978-355-4378
www.dharma.org/ims

San Francisco Zen Center
300 Page Street
San Francisco, CA 94102
415-863-3136
http://sfzc.org

Shambhala International
Halifax, Nova Scotia, Canada
902-425-4275
www.shambhala.org

Shambhala Mountain Center
Red Feather Lakes, Colo.
888-788-7221
www.shambhalamountain.org

White Plum Asanga
www.whiteplum.org

CULTIVATING MINDFULNESS AT WORK

Carroll, Michael. *Awake at Work: 35 Practical Buddhist Principles for Discovering Clarity and Balance in the Midst of Work's Chaos.* Boston: Shambhala, 2004.

Richmond, Lewis. *Work as a Spiritual Practice: A Practical Buddhist Approach to Inner Growth and Satisfaction on the Job.* New York: Broadway Books, 1999.

Whitmyer, Claude, ed. *Mindfulness and Meaningful Work: Explorations in Right Livelihood.* Berkeley, Calif.: Parallax Press, 1994.

STRATEGIES FOR EVERYDAY LIFE

Chödrön, Pema. *No Time to Lose: A Timely Guide to the Way of the Bodhisattva.* Boston: Shambhala Publications, 2005.

Kabat-Zinn, Jon. *Coming to Our Senses: Healing Ourselves and the World through Mindfulness.* New York: Hyperion, 2006.

Mipham, Sakyong. *Ruling Your World: Ancient Strategies for Modern Life.* New York: Morgan Road Books, 2005.

Sun Tzu. *The Art of War: The Denma Translation.* Boston: Shambhala, 2002.

Taylor, Rodney. *The Confucian Way of Contemplation: Okada Takehiko and the Tradition of Quiet-Sitting.* Columbia, S.C.: The University of South Carolina Press, 1988.

AUTHENTIC MANAGEMENT

Badaracco, Joseph L., Jr. *Leading Quietly: An Unorthodox Guide to Doing the Right Thing.* Boston: Harvard Business School, 2002.

Boyatzis, Richard, and Annie McKee. *Resonant Leadership: Renewing Yourself and Connecting with Others through Mindfulness, Hope, and Compassion.* Boston: Harvard Business School, 2005.

Cloke, Kenneth, and Joan Goldsmith. *The Art of Waking People Up: Cultivating Awareness and Authenticity at Work.* San Francisco: Jossey-Bass, 2003.

Easterbrook, Gregg. *The Progress Paradox: How Life Gets Better While People Feel Worse.* New York: Random House, 2003.

Frost, Peter J. *Toxic Emotions at Work: How Compassionate Managers Handle Pain and Conflict.* Boston: Harvard Business School, 2003.

Goleman, Daniel, Richard Boyatzis, and Annie McKee. *Primal Leadership: Realizing the Power of Emotional Intelligence.* Boston: Harvard Business School, 2002.

Hornstein, Harvey A. *Managerial Courage: Revitalizing Your Company without Sacrificing Your Job.* New York: Wiley, 1986.

Ryan, Kathleen D., and Daniel K. Oestreich. *Driving Fear Out of the Workplace: How to Overcome the Invisible Barriers to Quality, Productivity and Innovation.* San Francisco: Jossey-Bass, 1991.

Senge, Peter, C. Otto Scharmer, Joseph Jaworski, and Betty Sue Flowers. *Presence: Human Purpose and the Field of the Future.* Cambridge, Mass.: Society for Organizational Learning, 2004.

Sutton, Robert. *The No Asshole Rule: Building a Civilized Workplace and Surviving One That Isn't.* New York: Warner Business Books, 2007.

Wurman, Richard Saul. *Information Anxiety.* New York: Doubleday, 1989.

ESSAYS AND PAPERS ON APPLIED MINDFULNESS

Hallowell, Edward M. "Overloaded Circuits: Why Smart People Underperform." *Harvard Business Review,* January 2005.

Keeva, Steven W. "Practicing from the Inside Out." *Harvard Negotiation Law Review: Mindfulness in the Law and Alternative Dispute Resolution* 7 (Spring 2002).

Peppet, Scott R. "Can Saints Negotiate? A Brief Introduction to the Problems of Perfect Ethics in Bargaining." *Harvard Negotiation Law Review: Mindfulness in the Law and Alternative Dispute Resolution* 7 (Spring 2002).

Riskin, Leonard. "The Contemplative Lawyer: On the Potential Contributions of Mindfulness Meditation to Law Students, Lawyers and Their Clients." *Harvard Negotiation Law Review: Mindfulness in the Law and Alternative Dispute Resolution* 7 (Spring 2002).

Tolson, Jay. "Is There Room for the Soul? New Challenges to Our Most Cherished Beliefs about Self and the Human Spirit." *U.S. News & World Report,* October 23, 2006.

ORGANIZATIONS FOR APPLIED MINDFULNESS

The Center for Contemplative Mind in Society
Northampton, Mass.
413-582-0071
www.contemplativemind.org

Naropa University
Boulder, Colo.
800-772-6951
www.naropa.edu

The Penn Program for Stress Management
The University of Pennsylvania Health System
Philadelphia, Pa.
800-789-7366
www.uphs.upenn.edu/stress/about/index.html

Program on Negotiation at Harvard Law School
Harvard Negotiation Insight Initiative
Boston, Mass.
www.pon.harvard.edu/research/projects/hnii.php

The Shambhala Institute for Authentic Leadership
Halifax, Nova Scotia, Canada
902-425-0492
www.shambhalainstitute.org

Won Institute of Graduate Studies
Glensided, Pa.
215-884-8942
www.woninstitute.org

ABOUT THE AUTHOR

OVER HIS twenty-five-year business career, Michael Carroll has held executive positions with such companies as Shearson Lehman/American Express, Simon & Schuster, and the Walt Disney Company. The author of *Awake at Work,* he has an active consulting and coaching business with client firms such as Procter & Gamble, Comcast, Unilever, AstraZeneca, Aramark, Lutheran Medical Center, National Board of Medical Examiners, and others.

Michael has been studying Tibetan Buddhism since 1976, he graduated from Buddhist seminary in 1982, and he is a senior teacher in the Shambhala Buddhist lineage. He has lectured at Wharton Business School, Columbia University, Swarthmore College, St. Mary's University, Kripalu, Cape Cod Institute, Zen Mountain Monastery, Omega Institute (assisting Pema Chödrön), and other settings throughout the United States, Canada, and Europe.

For more information, visit www.awakeatwork.net.